First published in the United Kingdom in 2024 by the modernist, an independent not for profit organisation

Copyright © Nick Job 2024

All rights reserved. No part of this publication may be copied, displayed, extracted, reproduced, utilised, stored in a retrieval system or transmitted in any form or by any means, electronic, mechanical or otherwise, including but not limited to photocopying, recording or scanning without the prior written permission of the publisher.

The opinions expressed in this book are those of the author and should not necessarily be considered to be those of the publisher or its employees.

Designed by Nick Job

Typeset in Rail Alphabet 2, designed by Margaret Calvert and Henrik Kubel

Printed and bound in the United Kingdom by Pression

ISBN 978-1-7394927-3-1

The British Rail symbol (known as the Double Arrow) is a registered trade mark of the Secretary of State for the Department for Transport.

All illustrative examples of the British Rail Corporate Identity, including specific graphic devices from the Corporate Identity Manual, and any associated branding materials, are used with the permission of the Department for Transport.

The elements of the Network SouthEast brand, including the 'Namestyle', the 'Branding Strip' and the 'Triple Flash', are registered trademarks of the Network SouthEast Railway Society.

All photographs unless otherwise indicated Copyright © Nick Job

Every reasonable effort has been made by the author and publisher to seek permission for and attribute copyright material—including illustrations, designs and photography—used in this publication. However if such material has been inadvertently used without permission or acknowledgment we apologise and will attempt to make the necessary correction at the earliest opportunity.

Arrows of desire
Nick Job

Bring me my Bow of burning gold:
　　　Bring me my Arrows of desire:
Bring me my Spear: O clouds unfold:
　　　Bring me my Chariot of fire!

WILLIAM BLAKE (1757–1827)

Contents

	Foreword	7
	Cultural icon	8
	Introduction	13
1	Background	16
2	Arrival of a classic	20
3	Design analysis	22
4	Our continental friends	26
5	Perfect partners	28
6	Logotypography	32
7	Getting in shape	35
8	Upon reflection	38
9	Common errors	42
10	Manual miscellany	46
11	Significant outliers	50
12	Another dimension	54
13	Sectorisation	56
14	Local self-expression	61
15	Size matters	65
16	Low fidelity	66
17	One for the road	71
18	Civic duty	72
19	Up, up and away	74
20	Artistic licence	76
21	Look back in anger	78
22	The privatisation era	80
23	What if?	84
24	Back to the future	89
	Acknowledgments	94

← **British Rail pole sign at Coventry**
Wayne Fox

Foreword

It has been the privilege of my life to have headed both Transport for London (TfL) as Commissioner from 2006 to 2015, and Network Rail—currently the nearest thing to a national railway organisation—as Chair from 2015 until 2024. Not only because they, and the transport they operate, are an integral part of the economic, political, and social lives of London and Great Britain respectively, but because they both have a formidable and much loved design heritage. To be entrusted with what these organisations do is a challenge, but to care for and try to continue and improve their design heritage is a huge but pleasurable responsibility. Both organisations have a symbol and lettering, which together give an enduring image any commercial organisation would die for!

That's why I'm so pleased to see Nick Job's volume on the British Rail 'double arrow', and delighted to provide the foreword for it.

And the book comes at a crucial moment for Britain's railways. After several decades of balkanisation, the work Keith Williams has done on rail reform, informed by what passengers and customers want, emphasises that railway users see the railway as a network, seeking common standards of information, ticketing and an intelligible fares structure.

The double arrow, of course, has never left the public's consciousness as the mark of the nation's railway—used outside every station, and as the symbol for a station on Ordnance Survey and Google maps. It looks as fresh today as it did when it was first drawn by Gerry Barney sixty years ago, but is now destined to be used much more again in the future to emphasise a more cohesive approach to running our railways. Together with the refreshed railway typeface, Rail Alphabet 2, recently developed by Margaret Calvert and Henrik Kubel, our railway will shortly once again look like a coherent whole built around this design masterpiece.

Thanks to Nick's diligent work, you can trace the double arrow symbol from its origin, replacing some steam-age and rather basic attempts at heraldry (although, admittedly at least, using Gill Sans lettering for the most part), through many iterations, to its use today and tomorrow (which Nick himself has helped make sure is elegant and accurate). I hope you enjoy his work, and the story of the evolution of this remarkable and enduring symbol of the modern British railway.

Peter, Lord Hendy of Richmond Hill CBE
Minister of State for Rail, Department for Transport

← Curved stainless steel British Rail symbol at Leicester

Cultural icon

British Rail's 'double arrow' is an extraordinary survivor. The symbol has outlasted most of its kin, embedding itself in the public psyche—and in wider popular culture—in a manner unusual for transport trademarks and the like.

In the process the double arrow has moved beyond its original function of identifying British Rail into something larger and more diffuse, embodying the concept of rail travel in general. By now it has become a reliable and reassuring constant amongst the kaleidoscopic confusion of branding across the privatised railway, in which train operator names and visual identities chop and change.

It has also found an extraordinary second life away from the railway.

In itself, the double arrow exemplifies the simple joy good transport design can bring on its own terms. But my particular interest is in the way transport influences, and is reflected in, the arts and popular culture.

There can be few better examples of the double arrow's suffusion into the wider cultural space than its frequent appearance on football 'away day' stickers. These stickers, which seem to have proliferated in recent years, are applied by football fans when travelling (often but not always by train) to towns and cities for away matches. They can be found stuck to the inside of train carriages or on street furniture deep in rival territory and, intriguingly, usually feature surprisingly accurately rendered double arrow symbols within an apparently pre-ordained design. It is hard to know exactly why, but it may reflect the use of trains to reach away matches, referring back to the days of British Rail's notorious 'Footex' football special trains. One such sticker from Tarifa in southern Spain has made its way as far as the streets of Manchester and it too features a regulation double arrow, despite the fact that the symbol has little day-to-day relationship with either Spanish railways or Spanish football.

Spain's Renfe was nevertheless one of several state-owned railway operators to draw inspiration from British Rail's double arrow when devising its own logo, as this book explains. It seems obvious now—arrows are exactly what you would expect in a railway logo. But the concept wasn't obvious until the double arrow's creator Gerry Barney made it so.

Such arrows have spread beyond national railway systems and into entirely fictional ones. The immaculately branded LEGO® City public transport network uses a logo which combines the arrows first used in the British Rail symbol with the roundel of London's transport network (one of the few other transport symbols to survive in the way the double arrow has). It does so rather more successfully than the mural at King's Cross Thameslink station that you will read about in chapter 20. Promotional tie-ins for the Reverend Awdry's 'Railway Series' (the Thomas the Tank Engine books) from the 1970s featured a curved 'Sodor Rail' derivative of British Rail's own double arrow.

Transport-related tie-ins are one thing, but the double arrow has gone beyond that. One

Wealdstone FC sticker on the seawall at Cromer →
Chris Doward

clothing company which celebrates 'the nooks and crannies of popular culture' offers a full range of tops featuring the double arrow. Others sell socks etc. The symbol has in fact been adopted by discerning fashionistas for some time. Damon Albarn, lead singer of Britpop band Blur, stepped off a charter train at Glasgow Central in 2012 sporting a large red double arrow on his T-shirt while promoting the *Africa Express* music project. At that moment it became clear that the double arrow had transcended transport and been fully co-opted into the worlds of both fashion and the arts.

Artist Darren Almond turned the double arrow into a sculpture in 2005, and it was duly acquired by the Government Art Collection. There are fine art print publishers selling artistic interpretations of the double arrow, joining other 'ordinary' pieces of product design like Campbell's soup cans as subjects for artworks people want to hang on their walls.

But as well as being a neat and bold piece of graphic design with which to adorn their clothing or living spaces, the double arrow has real meaning to real people. There are political campaigns playing with the double arrow purely to evoke something people understand about the sort of railway system they want.

In becoming this cultural phenomenon, the double arrow has long outlived British Rail. Britain's railways were privatised in the mid-nineties, yet this symbol lives on. The industry has never found anything better to represent the nation's railways, although some railway organisations have, perhaps unwisely, tried to redesign it.

One final illustration of the timeless nature of the double arrow was a decision made by the volunteers who look after Attenborough station when they created a large 'bug hotel' for one of their platforms. The chosen design by Tim Sexton took as its inspiration the double arrow rather than any other graphic device from the post-privatisation railway network. For those volunteers, as for so many of us, it seems the double arrow encapsulates the railway far better than anything else.

The double arrow has escaped its original confines, permeated popular culture and is lodged in the collective consciousness as the true symbol for 'railway'. In this book, Nick does a sterling job explaining the double arrow's development, use and misuse, and the inherent quality that has ensured its survival.

The double arrow is quite simply an icon; a beautiful and important piece of design. And in a way it no longer belongs just to the railway industry, but to all of us. That is why its story deserves to be told in the pages that follow.

Daniel Wright
thebeautyoftransport.com

← Bobble hat by Mamnick of Sheffield
Thom Barnett

Introduction

This is a book about a logo—a logo that is dear to my heart, not only because of the way it looks but also for what it stands for—a logo that has the capacity to convey either unbridled anticipation or forlorn trepidation, depending on your opinion of what it represents and just how empty or full your glass happens to be when it comes to the notion of our railways in Britain. For to some this logo still stands for a largely late-running, grubby and unglamorous, increasingly disjointed service in dire need of significant investment, notoriously epitomised in the past by curling cheese sandwiches, the reputation of which not even national treasure Prue Leith could rescue. To others, the logo promises something far more exhilarating, namely the scope to breathe and to broaden one's horizons; a direct connection to the hustle and bustle of the metropolis or a passport to rural freedoms untold, whether in solitude or part of the crowd; either way an invitation into an alluring and unfolding wider world, demanding to be discovered and explored, conquered and exploited, utterly savoured and thoroughly loved.

My formative years in the late seventies and early eighties were spent in the idyllic but sleepy Peak District, just a stone's throw from Chatsworth House. Encounters with the railway were few and far between but always a very welcome and replenishing interruption to the pedestrian pace of life in the Derbyshire Dales. From time to time, visiting such family holiday destinations as Bournemouth and Ipswich would mean crossing mainlines in various places. Abbots Ripton and Steventon were favourite locations for maybe an hour or so of picnicking and railway gratification.

Occasional trips to Chesterfield station would also penetrate the tedium, usually to see off or welcome back older siblings to and from boarding school. The hurried purchase of the requisite 4p platform ticket was a distinct highlight, rewarded on the far side of the ticket barrier with that adrenaline-inducing first glimpse of Warning Yellow as the prestigious locomotive-hauled expresses hove into view. In later years the resounding roar of the Paxman Valenta engines at either end of the whispering carriages of the state-of-the-art Inter-City 125 would bring temporary deafness but sustained rhapsody. These experiences were all too brief, then a return to the mundane, where I would while away countless hours drawing 125s with my trusty Caran d'Ache colouring pencils, inspired by a short booklet about High Speed Trains that I had stumbled upon in a bookstall at Chatsworth Country Fair of all places.

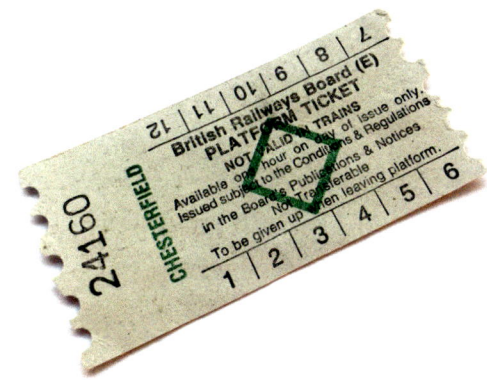

← British Rail Inter-City 125
Thomas Pye

In the summer of 1984, we moved to Rugby where, on the day of our arrival, I discovered the West Coast Main Line. Unpacking boxes could wait; *Caledonian* and *Cœur de Lion* would not. Rugby was a busy junction, averaging one train every four or five minutes. The electric trains would effortlessly glide by, albeit having to slow rather inconveniently to negotiate the unfavourable former track alignment through the late Victorian station, conveniently enough however for those like me to be able to read and absorb the impressive array of noteworthy nameplates that graced the Class 86 and 87 fleets. Normal West Coast Main Line operations would be punctuated each day by the passing APT (Advanced Passenger Train), fleetingly adding another welcome level of fascination to proceedings and causing me to be late home for tea on several occasions.

Off to boarding school I too would go in September 1984. Sometimes we would drive down the Fosse Way, but I would often travel by train from Rugby to Bath Spa, which involved changing at both Birmingham New Street and Bristol Temple Meads, two considerable hives of activity with more than enough railway action to captivate this wide-eyed youth.

When the time came to find lower sixth work experience, I wrote a letter to British Rail, specifically to the Architecture, Design and Environment department—more in hope than expectation—and was grateful to be offered a week's placement at their offices at Southern House in Croydon. There was not all that much for me to do there but nobody objected to the suggestion that I should be left to my own devices in their stockroom for a day or two where I was exposed for the first time to the British Rail Corporate Identity Manual and the sizeable library of supplementary Information Sheets. I helped myself to a copy of every page I could lay my hands on, having been positively encouraged to do so by a perplexed Head of Design, Tony Howard, who seemed more than happy to indulge my fascination, one that would eventually become an obsession.

In September 1991, having finished a year-long art foundation course at Mid-Warwickshire College in Royal Leamington Spa, I joined the Graphic Design degree course at Nottingham Trent University. There I was glad to have among my tutors two eminent designers: John Oldfield, who had worked in Norman Wilson's studio and was a key player in the development of a striking new corporate identity for the National Bus Company in 1972; and Chris Timings, an associate at Design Research Unit (DRU) who had designed the award-winning City of Westminster street nameplates in 1967. These two masters further fanned into flame my passion for corporate identity.

My first meaningful job came as a junior in-house graphic designer for the global logistics company Exel. After nearly a decade, and a couple of rebrands later, I had become guardian of the company's visual identity but, having few outlets for creative expression, jumped at the opportunity to embrace freelancing as a brand designer, simultaneously fulfilling a long-held ambition to design typefaces, a field which had interested me for several years.

During this time, my collection of British Rail branding materials steadily expanded and in 2011, with the generous permission of the

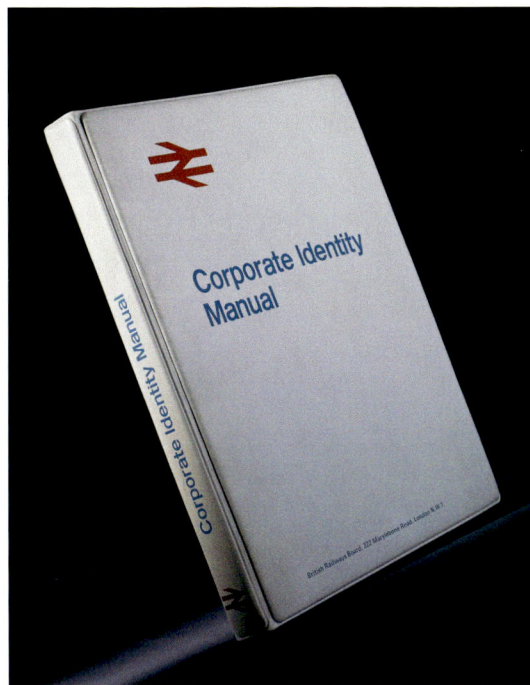

Wallace Henning/John Short

Department for Transport, much of the remarkable British Rail branding system was made available at *www.doublearrow.co.uk* where it can be fully appreciated by all. It was also a great privilege to be involved in Wallace Henning's superb Kickstarter project to publish the British Rail Corporate Identity Manual in hardback format, a must-have volume for any serious student of design.

As the cover of the Manual affirms, the mainstay of the British Rail Corporate Identity remains the symbol itself. Although I referred to it at the outset as a 'logo,' British Rail never actually called it that. Since things were done properly at 222 Marylebone Road, the British Railways Board preferred the more correct designation 'symbol', reserving the longer term 'logotype' for the words British Rail. The word 'logo' derives from the Greek λόγος (*logos*), which simply means 'word'. The essential beauty of the British Rail symbol, as with any memorable visual motif, is that words are simply not required.

My own preoccupation with the British Rail Corporate Identity can be easily put down to the fact that it lies squarely in the sweet spot between modernist design and railways, my partiality for which I have already confessed. The British Rail symbol is totemic of a nation of geographic and cultural variety, broad interest and endless possibilities, where, like the letters in a stick of seaside rock, it provides a thread that runs the length of the country, helping to hold it all together.

In a collection of concise and accessible chapters, I have drawn together an illustrative history of the British Rail symbol. From its emergence in 1964, I have traced its journey through various manifestations, for better and for worse, right up until the present day as the symbol faithfully continues to ply its trade well over half a century later, albeit in the context of an unbearably fractured railway—precisely the circumstances for which it was not conceived! In the closing chapters, I explore the potential future landscape for a revised symbol, based on a critique of the characteristics that I have tried to tease out in the earlier chapters of the book, which I hope you will enjoy.

Nick Job

1
Background

The so-called 'Big Four' railway companies—Great Western Railway (GWR), London, Midland and Scottish Railway (LMS), London and North Eastern Railway (LNER), and Southern Railway (SR)—were formed on 1 January 1923 by the grouping of 27 major railway companies and 94 subsidiaries, following the Railways Act 1921, an arrangement that was to last a quarter of a century. Soon after the Second World War, the Transport Act 1947, passed by Clement Attlee's Labour government, made provision for the nationalisation of Britain's railways. At midnight on 1 January 1948, the British Transport Commission (BTC) took over the assets of the Big Four and British Railways was born.

The financial position of British Railways gradually worsened until its first operating deficit was recorded in 1955. The elaborate Modernisation Plan, published in 1954 and projected to cost £1.2 billion, failed to stem the haemorrhage. Indeed by 1960 the company was suffering heavy losses with passenger and freight traffic both in sharp decline, due in no small part to the rapidly improving road network and the growing popularity of the motor car, a more convenient and increasingly affordable alternative to rail travel.

The Transport Act 1962 passed by Harold Macmillan's Conservative government led to the formation of the British Railways Board (BRB) on 1 January 1963. One of five newly formed public corporations, BRB assumed all of the railway related responsibilities of the BTC. Richard Beeching, who had been appointed chairman of the BTC in 1961, became the first chairman of the Board and continued to search for ways to reverse the fortunes of the railways. Though principally remembered for his 1963 report, *The Reshaping of British Railways*, along with the subsequent closure of almost a third of Britain's railway network, Dr Beeching's greatest legacy was arguably the creation of a single brand for the railways. He supervised the activities of the British Rail Design Panel, a working party originally formed by Sir Brian Robertson in 1956, which consisted of industrial designers and members of staff, whose main focus was on delivering a uniform and cohesive corporate image.

In February 1963, the Design Centre in London hosted a four-week exhibition entitled *New Design for British Railways*, curated by George Williams, Director of Industrial Design, showcasing the work of the Design Panel. Convinced that design could be a force for social good, Williams had previously been a product designer at Design Research Unit, Britain's first multi-disciplinary design agency, where he had become an associate and friend of founding member, Milner Gray, an influential voice as a consultant member of the Design Panel. The exhibition was a great success and gave Gray the firm conviction that the Board should consider a complete change of public image, a suggestion that was whole-heartedly embraced by Williams.

British Railways had until then been labouring under three largely unsatisfactory visual devices: The BTC favoured a lion astride a wheel **1.1**, a simplification of the official seal adopted after its formation in 1948, which soon became known as the 'starving lion' but was eschewed by the Railway Executive. They had preferred instead to use A J White's simpler 'totem' **1.2**, loosely based on Edward Johnston's celebrated London Transport roundel, albeit compressed and rounded, which added to its charm but warranted its nickname, the 'hotdog'. A third emblem **1.3** would emerge in 1953, an heraldic 'demi-lion rampant' holding a railway wheel above a coronet featuring the three national emblems—an English rose, a Scottish thistle and, for some reason, two Welsh leeks—arranged either side of a British oak leaf. The 'ferret and dartboard' was intentionally armorial in nature; indeed a grant of arms was obtained in 1956 but the crest was, if anything, even less remarkable than its two predecessors.

The members of the Design Panel were in general agreement that the basic feature still lacking on the railways was a single, cohesive house style. The imagery and colours being used were old-fashioned and entirely out of keeping for any modern, forward-looking business. Following the Board's approval, an internal steering committee was formed to focus on the design and implementation of a new visual style. Unsurprisingly it was DRU, having already delivered several projects for Beeching's Board, who were commissioned to give the nation's railways a much needed makeover. Their solution was groundbreaking in terms of its scale and scope; no organisation of its size had thus far attempted such an epic and far-reaching branding exercise.

1.1

1.2

1.3

And so the British Railways Board boldly embarked upon a comprehensive branding programme to breathe life into Britain's failing and neglected rail industry. Codified in four volumes, using the MULT-O 23-ring binder system, the British Rail Corporate Identity Manual was compiled by Ellis Miles, Design Officer, and would become the touchstone for all aspects of the new image. Such was its success that requests for copies were received from as far afield as the Americas and Japan.

The basic elements of the Corporate Identity—the symbol, an accompanying sans serif typeface called Rail Alphabet and a vibrant colour palette, featuring a contemporary interpretation of Britain's traditional red, white and blue—would be applied with vigour to the entire system, bringing much needed brand conformity across all railway related activities, including publicity, uniforms, signage and livery for trains, ships and road vehicles.

The linchpin of this ambitious project was the innovative symbol, the distinctive signature of a streamlined organisation now known by a shorter, more versatile name: British Rail. Its first exposure came in the summer of 1964 on the cab-side of a Brush Type 4 locomotive as part of British Rail's XP64 concept train (see opposite) but was hastily removed and not seen again in public until the Corporate Identity was officially launched in January 1965 at another exhibition hosted by the Design Centre, entitled *The new face of British Railways* **1.4**.

Though widely acclaimed as a thing of aesthetic beauty and integrity, inevitably the symbol initially had its detractors, who variously described it as a 'lightning bolt', 'crow's feet', 'a

Mike Ashworth

piece of twisted barbed wire', and the politically barbed 'arrows of indecision'. Nevertheless it was here to stay, the stylish and yet timeless identifier of a forward-looking company, issuing a bold statement of intent as it embraced the future; a symbol to usher in the modern era for British Rail, one of renewed hope in Britain's railways—the age of the train.

18 Railway journals from July 1964 featuring the XP64 concept train →

2
Arrival of a classic

The famous symbol which came to replace the miscellany of ill-fitting forerunners was drawn by Gerry Barney, a lettering artist who had joined DRU in 1961 from Ealing Art School. Although Barney himself attached no specific interpretation to the design, the Corporate Identity Manual forthrightly informs us that the British Rail symbol 'consists of two-way traffic arrows on parallel lines representing tracks'. For what it is worth, trains, like road vehicles, have always travelled on the left in Britain, a vestige from a time when strangers would pass each other on the left, keeping the right hand free if necessary to brandish sword or dagger in the event of conflict; a similar principle applied in combat both in chariots and on horseback. The configuration of the symbol neatly observes the age-old custom of keeping left but who would have suspected any connection with self-defence or jousting?

Some six decades later, the story behind the genesis of the symbol is not especially clear cut. In the absence of finding a suitable solution after reviewing an initial round of concepts, DRU management unusually invited its entire staff to submit ideas for a new emblem and received more than fifty proposals, which were presented to Milner Gray of DRU and George Williams of BRB to be whittled down first to six, then two: Barney's familiar double arrow **2.1** and another abstract design, drawn by DRU graphic designer Collis Clements, a neat arrangement of two overlapping rings with an arrow pointing right to suggest forward motion **2.2**, the overall composition of which had the disadvantage of being distinctly one-directional.

Today several losing submissions remain in circulation and it is not implausible that four of the alternatives often cited in conjunction with this curious selection process **2.3** may well have been those that made up the final cohort of six.

What happened next is a matter of intrigue: In a late twist of fate—so the story goes—the preferred version put forward by Clements was inadvertently leaked to the press prior to the official launch and consequently dropped by the Board, ensuring Barney's proposal was promoted to first choice by default. Of course, Barney may not remember it quite that way. After all, why should he?

By Barney's own admission, the conception of the double arrow was short and sweet, hastily sketched on a scrap of paper whilst on the tube to work, the archetypal 'back-of-an-envelope-job'. Indeed he would only formalise it within a grid when he arrived at the office after his commute that morning.

As far as the design genre is concerned, symbols consisting of straight lines and arrows were not without precedent in the railway industry: It has been suggested for example that both F H K Henrion's vaunted interlocking twin chevrons for the Glasgow Electric 'Blue Train' service **2.4**, and the ingenious three-dimensional box and arrow designed by DRU's Ronald Sandiford for Rail Freight [sic] **2.5**, may have influenced Barney's design or at least brought it within reach.

3
Design analysis

Around the same time that modernism was beginning to make its indelible mark on British culture, there arose a preoccupation with optics in graphic design that would heavily influence the direction taken by DRU, impacting the evolution of the symbol in two subtle but significant ways:

Firstly, if drawn with parallel pairs of lines throughout to achieve mathematically constant stroke thickness, the outer arms of the design appeared to taper towards their extremes. To counter this illusion, the arms were adjusted so that they flared outwards slightly **3.1**, giving the impression of consistent weight throughout.

Secondly, it had been observed that a dark object on a light background appears thinner and lighter in weight, than its counterpart reversed out of a dark background **3.2**. In order to counter this effect, known as halation— namely the escaping of light beyond its proper boundaries—DRU prescribed two optically balanced versions of the British Rail symbol for use on both light and dark backgrounds **3.3**, the geometry of each defined by a 48 × 30 (8:5) construction grid (see opposite).

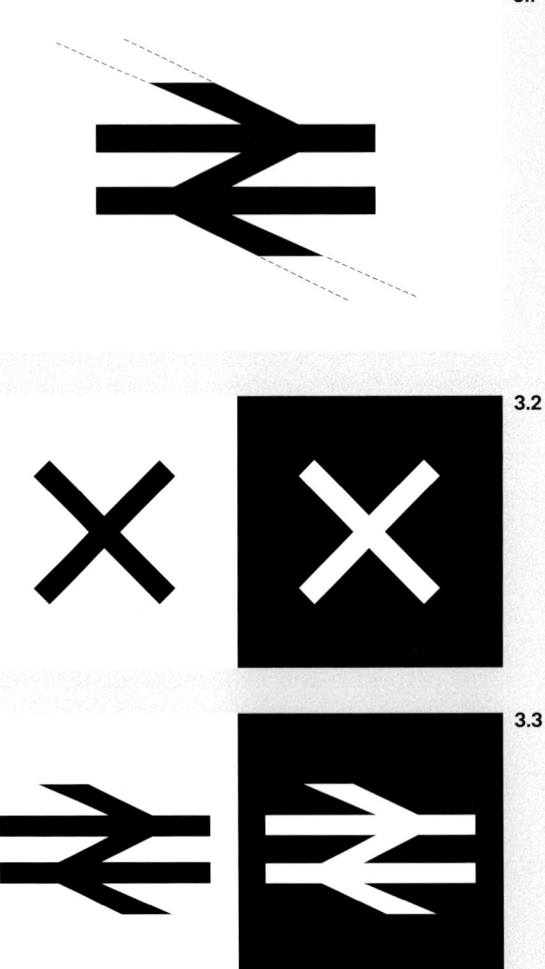

Construction grids for positive and negative versions of the British Rail symbol →

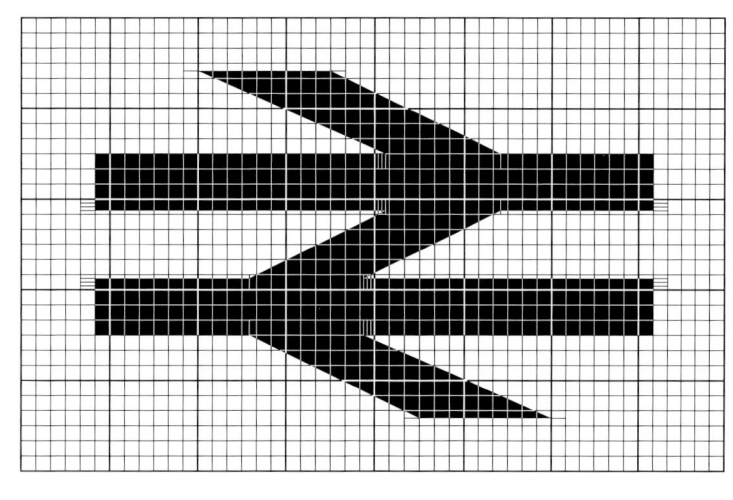
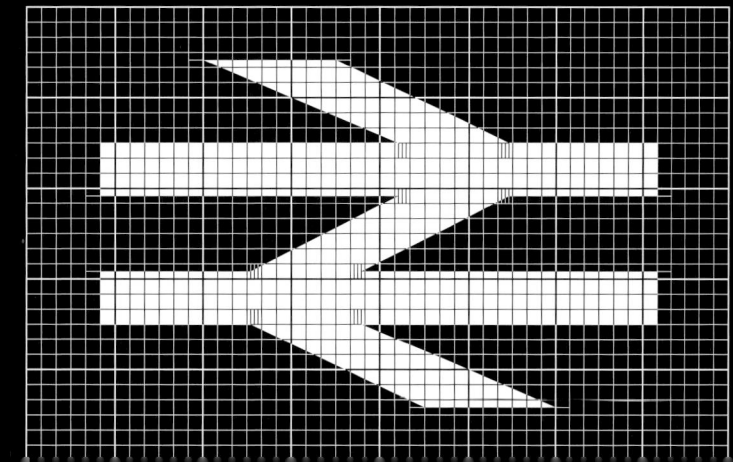

3.4

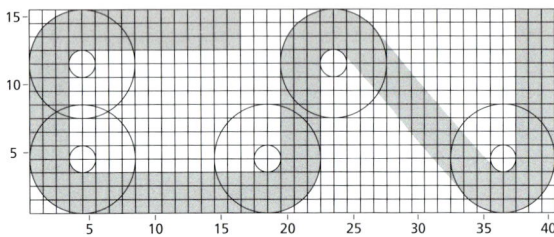

3.5

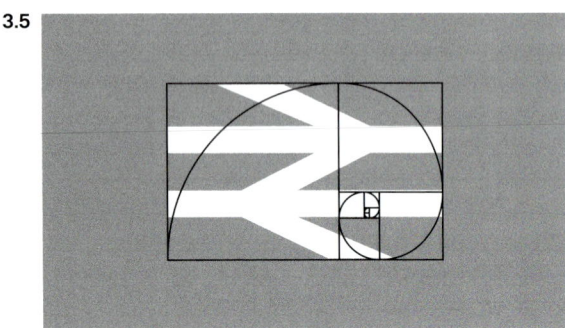

Mathematical grids were not yet *en vogue* and so the influence of a notable trail-blazing forebear, Allan Fleming's heavily constructed CN monogram **3.4**, introduced by Canadian National Railways in 1960, should not be overlooked. The principle of being able to reproduce the logo faithfully out in the wild with only basic drawing tools and a set of clear instructions would apply equally to the British Rail symbol which, on the surface of things, was nothing more than an array of 20 points joined together by 20 straight lines.

Many have come to appreciate the inherent genius of Barney's superlative symbol; its disarming simplicity; the fine balance it strikes between reassuring authority and assured confidence; the pleasing purity of its purely coincidental golden ratio proportions **3.5**; and, above all, its captivating memorability.

The symbol was an ideal fit for British Rail; it lacked the stuffy pretensions of grandeur associated with much of the imagery of railway companies past and was equally at home at all points on the vast spectrum of British railway architecture; ancient or modern, urban or rural, modest or magnificent.

In summary, the British Rail symbol just looked right; an ode to all that is excellent, noble and true across the broad expanse of design in the modern era. And it remains a faithful testimony to Barney's keen artistic eye and expert ability to formalise its proportions to achieve a lasting imprint upon all who behold its unmistakable form.

British Rail symbol above the entrance to Huddersfield station →

4
Our continental friends

Such was the immediate impact of the new symbol that British Rail became the envy and inspiration of several of its continental railway counterparts. As Oscar Wilde famously wrote, 'Imitation is the sincerest form of flattery that mediocrity can pay to greatness' and close examination of the visual devices adopted by Nederlandse Spoorwegen (Dutch Railways) **4.1**, SBB CFF FFS (Swiss Federal Railways) **4.2** and Renfe (Spanish National Railway Network) **4.3**—by no means an exhaustive list of emulators—reveals many underlying similarities, notably the lines of transverse motion reinforced by bold directional arrows, all reliably defined by precise and flawless geometry.

The prevalence of such prescriptive construction diagrams of varying complexity would suggest that mathematics reigned supreme in this particular discipline. When it came to logos however, the eye remained the final arbiter on all design matters; the master grid was merely slave to aesthetics, ensuring universal compliance by leaving the layman without excuse for not drawing precisely what the original designer had in mind on each and every occasion.

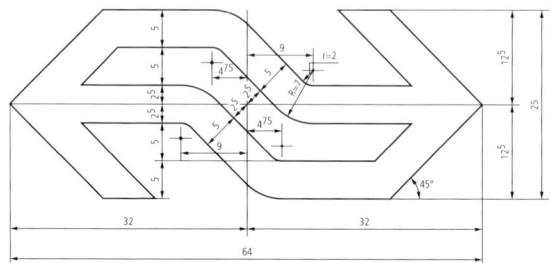

4.2

4.3

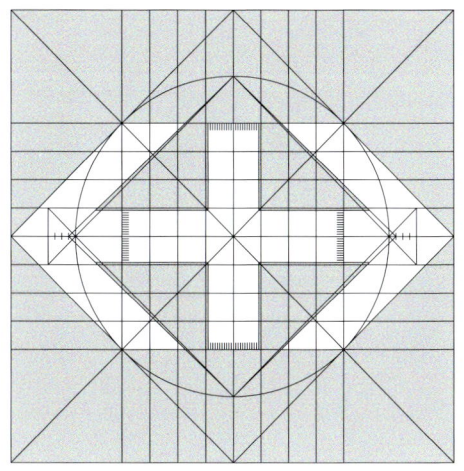

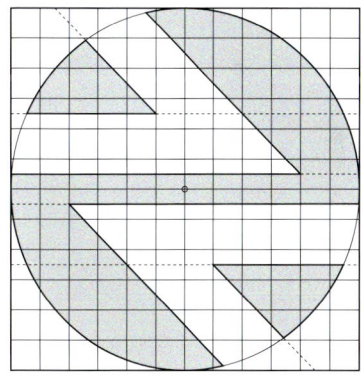

27

5
Perfect partners

When the time came to create a typeface to accompany the new British Rail symbol, DRU engaged the services of former employee and long-time associate Jock Kinneir, an eminent type designer and trusted expert in the field of lettering and legibility. Together with Margaret Calvert, his former student at Chelsea School of Art and now his junior design partner, Kinneir had already successfully delivered the lettering for the Ministry of Transport's ubiquitous traffic signs, pioneered on Britain's first motorway, the Preston bypass, which opened in December 1958 and now forms part of the M6.

Their smart solution, a bespoke sans serif typeface called Transport, was loosely based on Akzidenz-Grotesk, a popular German typeface from the turn of the century, seasoned with many subtle but necessary adjustments to improve legibility. The lettering was put through its paces in a series of rigorous simulations by the Road Research Laboratory, overcoming stiff competition from a slab serif upper-case model by letter-cutter David Kindersley, due in part to the theory that words set in upper and lower case are easier to read at distance than their upper-case equivalents.

Two weights of the typeface—Transport Medium **5.1** and Transport Heavy **5.2**—were drawn by Calvert for use on dark and light backgrounds respectively, thus giving visual equality of character in both scenarios. The letters were sensitively crafted and carefully spaced with each character positioned on an individual tile of fixed width.

It had been the intention to use the same typeface for British Rail and so Transport was tested in a number of railway environments, most notably in 1962 at the rebuilt railway station in Coventry where it was incorporated into the signage system. However Kinneir and Calvert convincingly argued that because the original performance requirements of the Transport typeface were very different—being able to read a legend quickly at long distance whilst driving at high speed is by no means the same proposition as effective wayfinding in a far less demanding pedestrian context—a sans serif typeface closer to the modern and appealing neo-grotesque model should be adopted for British Rail signage.

Conveniently Kinneir and Calvert had been working for the National Health Service on just such a typeface to bring greater efficiency and uniformity to signs across Britain's hospitals. Health Alphabet **5.3** was fashioned specifically with pedestrians in mind. And so there seemed every sensible reason to deploy the same basic letterforms for the British Rail project. With its many proven virtues, the typeface was duly proposed, promptly approved and pressed into service under a new name—Rail Alphabet.

The same typeface would also be used by the Ministry of Defence and later featured in the British Airports Authority sign system **5.4**.

5.1 ABCDEFGHIJKLMNOPQRST
UVWXYZabcdefghijklmnopqr
stuvwxyz1234567890¼½¾⅓⅔
()-:.,'-"//£%&? →

5.2 ABCDEFGHIJKLMNOPQRST
UVWXYZabcdefghijklmnopqr
stuvwxyz1234567890¼½¾⅓⅔
()-:.,'-"//£%&? →

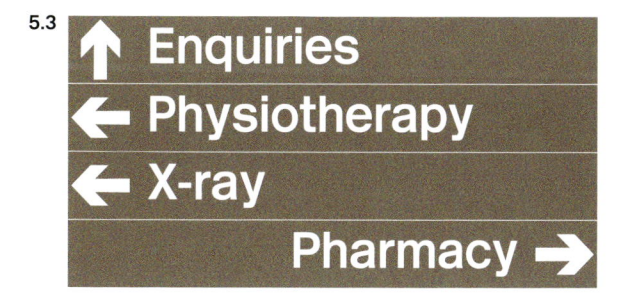

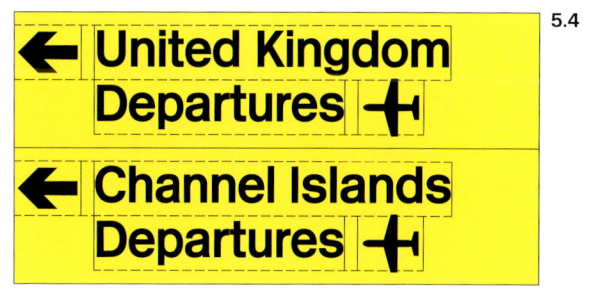

5.3
↑ Enquiries
← Physiotherapy
← X-ray
Pharmacy →

5.4
← United Kingdom Departures ✈
← Channel Islands Departures ✈

5.4

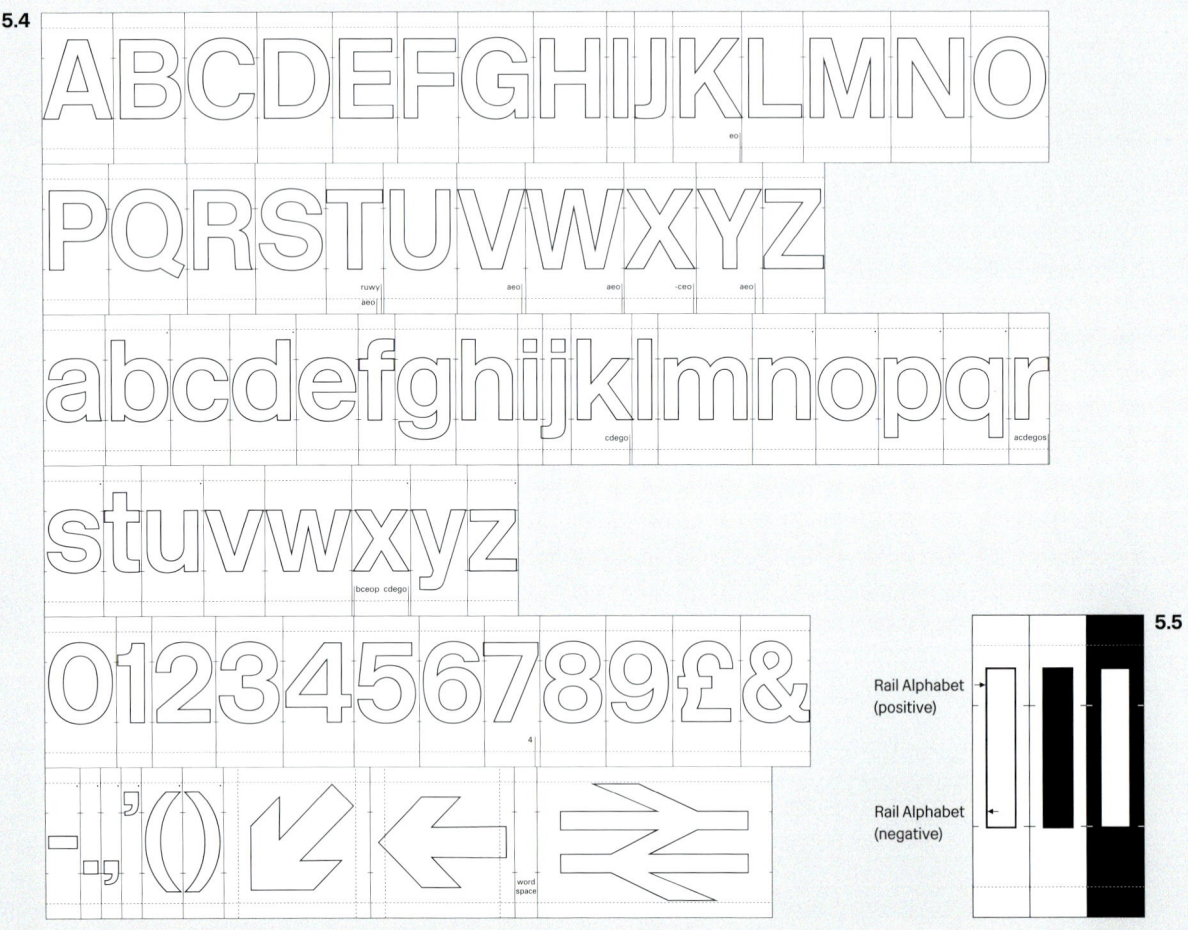

5.5 Rail Alphabet (positive) / Rail Alphabet (negative)

5.6 **Market Harborough**

As any respectable typeface designer will explain, legibility has as much to do with the spacing between letters as the design of the letterforms themselves. To enable consistent spacing, Rail Alphabet incorporates a tiling system **5.4** similar to that used in the Transport typeface. By remaining committed to their tried and tested method of spacing by using tiles of fixed widths, Kinneir and Calvert ensured that even untrained staff had a reasonable chance of assembling lettering correctly on signs.

Rail Alphabet is measured over the lower-case x-height, the height of the horizontal tracks of the British Rail symbol. Tile widths are specified for lettering with an x-height of 80, 100 and 120mm. Where more than one value is given, the tile width varies, depending on the adjoining character. The distance between lines is determined by butting tiles together on the broken lines to ensure that line-spacing is equal to the x-height. A dot is shown in the top right hand corner of any tiles which may accidentally be used upside-down. All text is set in upper and lower case and ranged left with only a few exceptions in certain signage scenarios.

Like the British Rail symbol, Rail Alphabet exists in positive and negative formats **5.5** but, unlike Transport, tile sizes are identical for both weights. The positive version of Rail Alphabet is represented by the outer edge of the outline of each character and is used for dark lettering on a light background; the negative version of Rail Alphabet is conversely represented by the inner edge of the outline of each character and is used for light lettering on a dark background.

The individual characters are neutral and unpretentious, following the Continental typographic traditions of the 1950s. However Kinneir and Calvert instilled their own character and charm into the typeface, deviating from Helvetica in the direction of Akzidenz-Grotesk, when there was deemed to be some ambiguity between certain characters.

Rail Alphabet was the perfect partner for the British Rail symbol **5.6**. Modern, clean and efficient, it was everything British Rail aimed to be. The hallmarks of the typeface, like the symbol, were simplicity and clarity. Its soft, organic contours provided the perfect foil for the clinical, straight-edged outlines of the symbol. The combination of visual elements was design *yin-yang* at its sublime best.

6
Logotypography

The British Rail logotype had three variants in both positive and negative formats **6.1**, two of which confined the British Rail symbol to a box derived from the standard 48 × 30 (8:5) grid. Many such British Rail logotypes, for example Railfreight **6.2**, were formulated in this way, sometimes with a splash of colour—generally Flame Red—to provide an orderly contingent of sub-brands, each one demonstrably from the same corporate stable.

    Surprisingly a slightly different set of lettering was used for logotypes. Typeset by hand, the letterforms were often finessed and the spacing tightened to give better visual results **6.3**. The differences are more apparent in some letters than others; most notably the lower-case 'a' diverges from the Rail Alphabet model, becoming more sympathetic to the inner curves of the 's' **6.4**.

    The symbol was vertically centred on the lower-case x-height, initially at a distance of one cap-height. This was later reduced by half (c.1980) to make a closer visual connection between symbol and logotype **6.5**. From that point onwards, versions with the symbol and logotype in a box were not thought to be 'boxing clever' and phased out, though not in all cases. The colourful Railair Link logotype **6.6** retained all three of its boxes and remains all the more charming because of it.

6.1

6.2

6.3
6.4
6.5
6.6
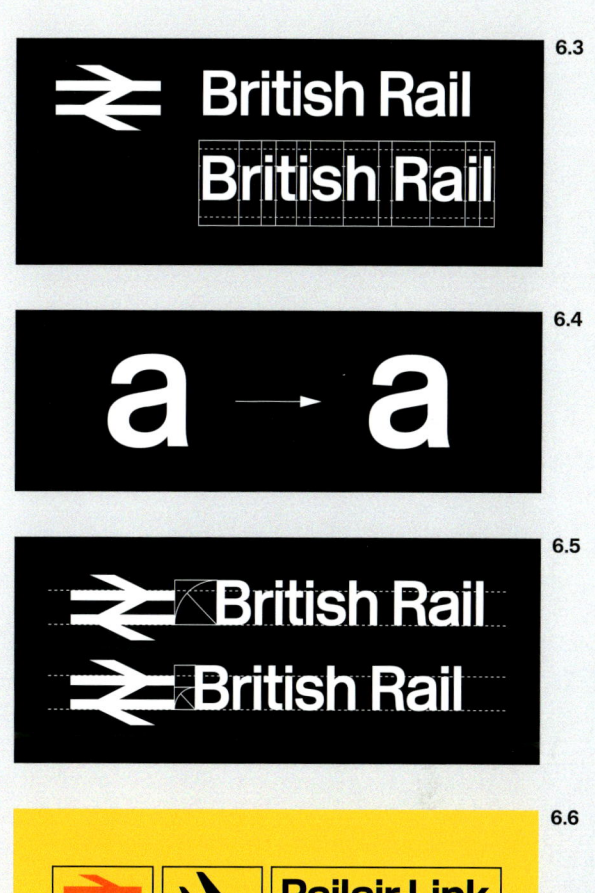

7
Getting in shape

Modern design theory tends to discourage the confinement of a corporate logo within another shape but the precedent for thus enclosing the British Rail symbol was set on the occasion of its first public outing, when it briefly appeared on the cab-side of D1733 set within a Flame Red square (see page 19).

    As noted in the previous chapter, for many years it was permissible to print the symbol within a rectangular box **7.1**, the inner edge of which was defined by the 8:5 exclusion zone. However, as we have observed, this particular treatment largely fell out of favour in the early eighties when the distance between symbol and logotype was reduced by half.

    Introduced in 1968, the British Rail Catering logotype consisted of a symbol surrounded by a thin circle, the radius of which was equal to the width of the symbol **7.2**. This arrangement adversely affected the established relationship between symbol and x-height. The circular format was applied in a systematic way to all British Rail catering establishments **7.3**. It is not clear why the catering division (later branded Travellers-Fare) was afforded its own circular emblem so early in the life of the Corporate Identity. Maybe the suggestion of a tender and succulent, medium-rare British Rail symbol upon a luxurious fine china dining plate was intended to evoke the opulent *haute cuisine* of the magnificent dining cars of yesteryear?

7.1

7.2

7.3

← **British Rail uniform buttons**
Luke Davydaitis

35

7.4

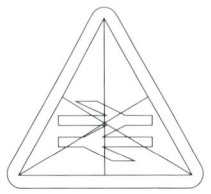

7.5
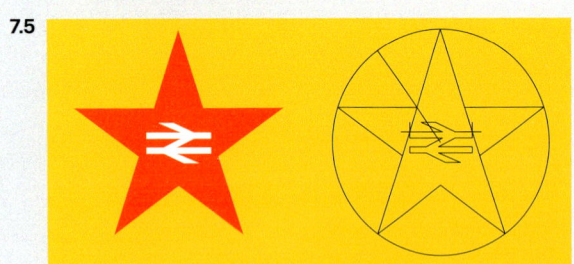

7.6

7.7

    The Accident Prevention Service (later the Safety Advisory Service), the department of British Rail dedicated to maintaining safety on the railway, adopted a Warning Yellow triangle with a black British Rail symbol and border **7.4**. The x-height of the associated logotype was vertically aligned with the symbol, which was positioned a little lower than the mathematical centre of the triangle, which would allow for a larger symbol, resulting in greater impact.

    Red Star, the registered parcel delivery service operated by British Rail, made use of scheduled trains to transport parcels between passenger stations across the rail network, providing a faster, more efficient alternative to Royal Mail. The service was first introduced in 1963 but became a casualty of privatisation and was eventually sold in 1999. The original Red Star logo **7.5** was constructed from a regular five-pointed star with the British Rail symbol placed at its mathematical centre. A contrived 'strobe' version **7.6** was introduced in 1986 and included two-, three- and even six-shadow variants. This time the British Rail symbol was positioned much nearer to the vertical centre of the star and enlarged close to breaking point within the star, an attempt to increase its presence within this more complex but less satisfactory composition.

    A related branding device was applied to MagStar **7.7**, the magazine distribution service launched in 1987, using an outlined two-shadow star complete with a dozen grey horizontal go-faster stripes, the kind of effect that had not previously been embraced as an appropriate branding treatment and something that would not have passed muster in the early days.

Great Yarmouth

8
Upon reflection

When it came to the orientation of the British Rail symbol, the Corporate Identity Manual was unequivocal: 'The top arrow points to the right.' There were two authorised exceptions to this rule, where it became expedient to mirror the symbol; firstly for flags, secondly for shipping purposes. There also existed an intersection between those two worlds, when flags were flown from ships.

And so a reflected version was permitted firstly for British Rail house flags, where the Manual explains: 'Top arrow of symbol points to flagstaff on both sides.' This would lead to a peculiarity which caught my attention in the *Observer's Book of Flags* by William Crampton, in which every flag—British Rail included—was displayed with the hoist to the left of the flag, whereby the symbol was shown quite correctly mirrored on the page but looking for all the world like an error.

The design of the house flag **8.1** was very straightforward; a Flame Red field in simple 2:1 proportions upon which was centred a white British Rail symbol, observing the standard 8:5 grid. The flag used for British Rail shipping was identical in every regard except it was Rail Blue and available in fewer sizes.

British Rail flags were single-sided affairs, manufactured from a resilient, synthetic fabric with the negative version of the symbol double-stitched into it. The decision to specify single sheet thickness had economic and practical benefits: There were clear financial savings to be made by only using half the material but it was also about performance—how well the flag would fly from the hoist. Although the Design Panel would have been typically zealous in applying the symbol consistently in every circumstance, a flag manufactured from two sheets of fabric to ensure that the symbol was displayed correctly on both sides, especially in the hard-wearing and relatively heavy gauge of polyester selected by British Rail, would not have the same capacity to billow satisfactorily when flown above stations, offices, depots and works. The largest house flag available was specified at 18 × 9 feet; the National Railway

8.2

Museum possesses an even larger specimen measuring 24 × 12 feet. Such behemoths were intended to be flown from the tallest company buildings—those where the finial stood 60 feet or more above ground—which tended to be the grander, more prestigious structures, where getting the image right was paramount. If one will pardon the pun, a limp, lacklustre flag would simply not fly at such railway cathedrals as Bristol Temple Meads and Doncaster Works. After all, no-one really wants a flagging flag. And thus the symbol was permitted to appear reflected on house flags.

 Whilst on this topic, a single-colour stylised depiction of the British Rail flag—as seen on the cover of this volume—was used on various promotional items pertaining especially to the Corporate Identity, published by the Director of Industrial Design during the mid-eighties **8.2**. In spite of the aforementioned concession to the British Rail flag, this compelling graphic was only ever used in printed matter as shown, that is to say, always bled off the right edge of the page. Mirroring this graphic would naturally have resulted in the British Rail symbol appearing the wrong way round, something that would have been strictly forbidden in marketing collateral. Bearing more than a passing resemblance to the old P&O logo **8.3**, especially in its proud, billowing nature, complete with flamboyant flick of the lower corner of the fly, the printed flag motif may have been a doff of the cap to the company's former shipping glories.

8.3

8.4

8.5

8.6

Matthew Murtland

Matthew Murtland

8.7

40

The story behind the reflected version of the symbol used by British's Rail shipping division **8.4** is rather more complicated. One myth that has been perpetuated for too long is that the reversed version of the British Rail symbol accommodates an 'S' for Sealink, so this version is often mistakenly referred to as the Sealink logo, a convenient narrative that suits those who feel the need to differentiate Sealink from British Rail. In reality the Sealink logotype shared the same basic format as all other British Rail sub-brands at the time, albeit with a light blue symbol as shown in the Corporate Identity Manual **8.5**.

Whilst a reflected symbol was used on the port side of the funnel **8.6**, it should be pointed out that the symbol used on the starboard side was still the regular version, as worn by the MV St Edmund in the Manual **8.7**. This all rather debunks the apocryphal 'S' for Sealink theory.

For a more rational explanation, one must acquaint oneself with a long-standing maritime convention whereby emblems on funnels are to point towards the bow of the vessel, a useful safety feature, especially in extremely busy shipping lanes where visibility may also be compromised by poor weather conditions. By adopting a reflected symbol on the port funnel, it became instantly clear to those in other vessels—once they had learned the rule that the top arrow always points forwards—which way a British Rail vessel was facing and therefore its likely direction of travel.

This approach would have provided the added benefit of brand consistency on any given vessel: If the symbol on the funnel were pointing forward, it would then be consistent with the British Rail house flag, which would naturally trail behind the hoist and thus both symbols would always point in the same direction regardless of which elevation was in view. Few if any photographs from the era in question show British Rail flags being flown on board vessels but the argument nevertheless remains cogent.

The principle of having a mirrored symbol on one side of ships eventually became so entrenched that even double-ended vessels such as the vehicle ferries used on the Isle of Wight and estuarial routes—those that moved back and forth without turning around—still displayed a reflected version on one side despite not really having a front to which the symbol could consistently point.

British Rail archives reveal that James Cousins, head of the Design Panel and successor to George Williams as Director of Industrial Design, evidently pushed for the symbol to be right-reading on both sides of vessels but his intention was met with firm resistance from the shipping management of the day, who were wholly unwilling to budge on what was seen as an essential safety feature and were no doubt not in the business of being told what their ships ought to look like by landlubbers from head office. And so the concession was made; the reflected symbol had prevailed—on the port-side of boats at least—until the shipping business was sold off by British Rail in 1984.

9
Common errors

For various reasons, examples of incorrectly drawn versions of the British Rail symbol were unfortunately all too commonplace across the network. The British Rail Corporate Identity Manual intentionally tackled three main threats to accurate reproduction:

(1) *Weight* – Since the symbol exists in two distinct formats for both positive and negative usage, a predictably frequent mistake was the application of the symbol in the wrong weight. It may not be obvious to the untrained eye but using the wrong version will clearly lead to one of two unsatisfactory outcomes; either the positive symbol appearing too light or the negative symbol too heavy **9.1**. It could be argued that British Rail made a rod for its own back by having two different versions of the symbol (not to mention alphabet and logotypes) and that topic will be discussed in greater detail in the penultimate chapter of the book. Suffice it to say for now that the British Rail design department were right to be concerned in this matter and, whilst the Corporate Identity Manual explicitly warned of this potential pitfall, it soon became abundantly clear that too many were unable to appreciate, remained oblivious to, or simply ignored, this technical and esoteric design facet.

(2) *Orientation* – Since the symbol does not have linear symmetry, the orientation of the symbol—closely examined in the previous chapter—was always likely to be a pinch-point. Although the instruction concerning the direction of the top arrow was crystal clear, there remained countless examples of the symbol frequently appearing back-to-front in various wayfinding situations **9.2**, attributable to either visual illiteracy or photographic errors in the production process. There was once a time when British Rail paid close attention to the correct orientation of the symbol on signage. Stand-alone totems and wall-mounted projecting boxes, such as those installed at Nantwich **9.3** and Exeter Central **9.4**, were generally constructed using a double-sided arrangement to ensure that the symbol would be right-reading on both sides. However, with no-one responsible nowadays for the overall policing of the symbol on the ground, the rule of handedness, particularly in the sphere of station branding, often falls by the wayside. Present-day examples of station identifiers at Ipswich **9.5** and London Bridge **9.6** show a regrettable lack of brand rigour when viewed from the 'wrong' direction.

9.1

9.4

9.2

9.5

9.3

9.6

Tim Dunn

43

9.7 Incorrect – parallel arms appear to taper   Correct – optically adjusted arms appear parallel

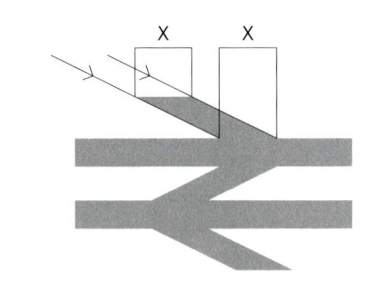

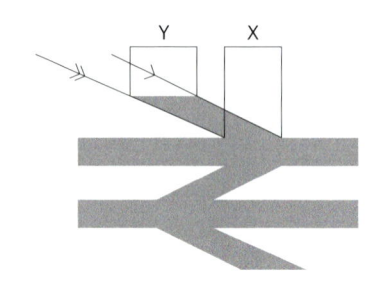

9.8

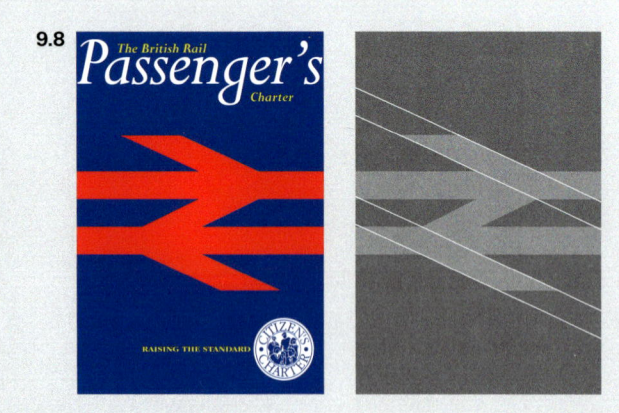

9.9

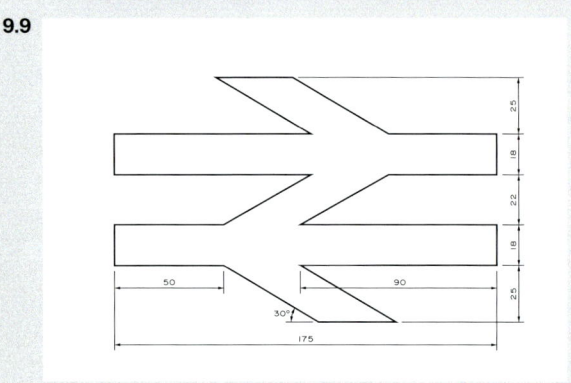

(3) *Parallel arms* – The seemingly intuitive approach of constructing the arms of the symbol with parallel lines gives the impression that they taper towards their extremities **9.7**. The Corporate Identity Manual highlighted this optical illusion: 'Note that the outer arrows broaden slightly towards their tips. If incorrectly drawn parallel they appear to taper outwards.' As noted in chapter 3, Barney took great care to ensure that the arms would appear the same thickness throughout, a nuance that eluded the designer of *The British Rail Passenger's Charter* (1992) **9.8**. The challenge of drawing the arms accurately is further illustrated in *Design Drawing One* by John Rolfe (English Universities Press/Hodder Arnold, 1975), the first in a series of three educational textbooks, containing simple exercises for the student of technical drawing. Rolfe's symbol **9.9** perpetuates the commonly held but mistaken belief that the arms should be constructed from parallels. Rolfe's measurements, including his aspect ratio of 175:108, are also the stuff of fantasy but that is not really the relevant point here.

Railman's hat manufactured by Compton Webb (Headdress) Limited in 1985 →

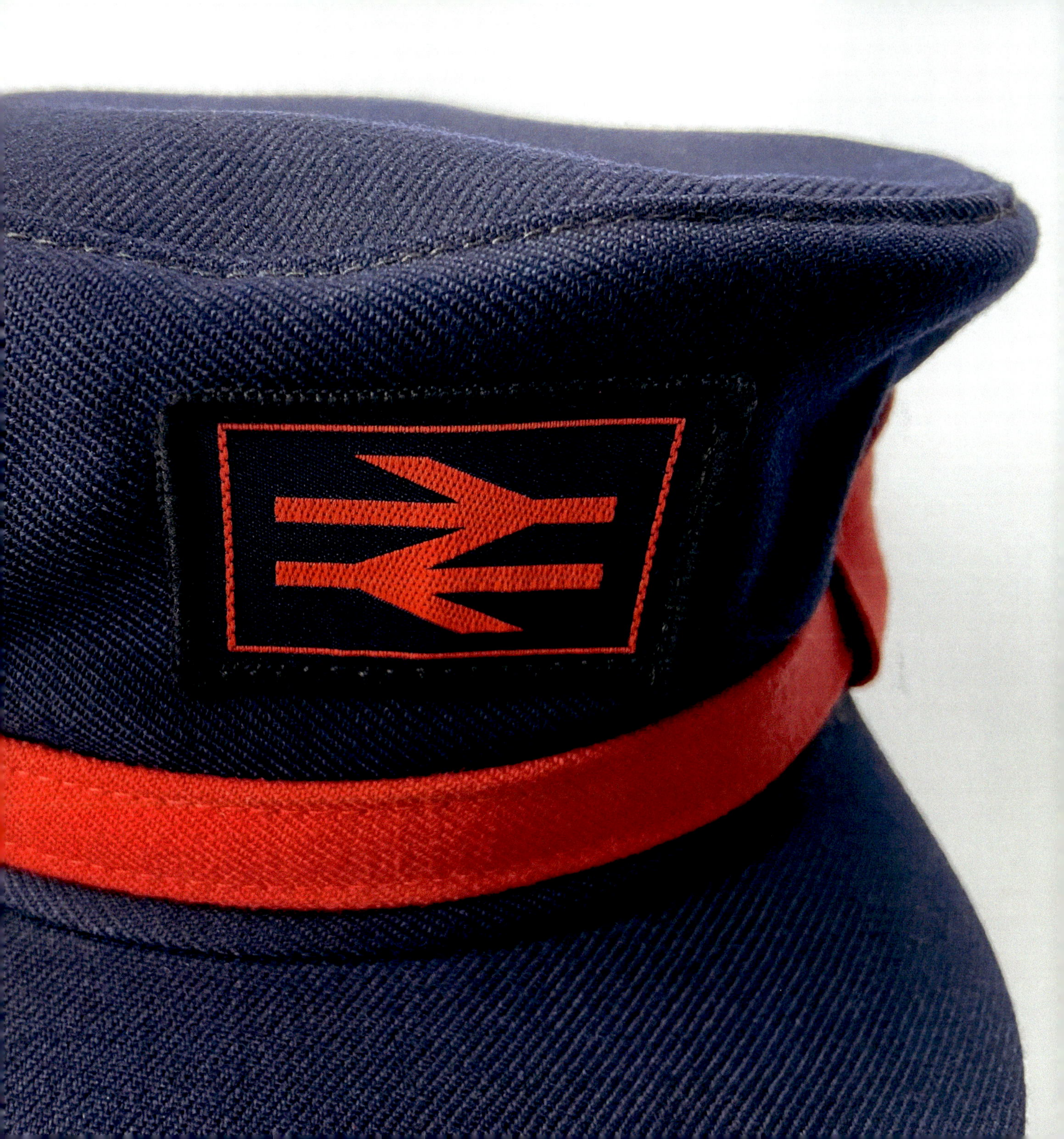

10
Manual miscellany

This chapter briefly examines some of the more unusual yet fully authorised treatments of the British Rail symbol, each one proudly taking its place in the pages of the British Rail Corporate Identity Manual.

The outline version of the symbol **10.1** was used more extensively in the early days of British Rail, furnishing the covers of many a timetable in the late sixties and early seventies. It is not apparent why an outline version was needed; it is difficult to imagine any specific requirement that could not be equally or better fulfilled by using a solid symbol.

The Advanced Passenger Train (APT) was a tilting high speed train developed by British Rail in the seventies and eighties. The project relied initially on gas turbine technology but later moved to overhead AC electric power with the intention of running a fleet of APTs on the fully electrified West Coast Main Line. The symbol created for the APT **10.2** differed from the outline version, being heavier in appearance and having rounded corners to match the specially drawn lettering for the logotype. On this occasion the distance between the symbol and the legend was reduced in keeping with the tighter lettering, which coalesced like quicksilver. As was typical of most British Rail logotypes, the artwork was supplied in both positive and negative formats **10.3**.

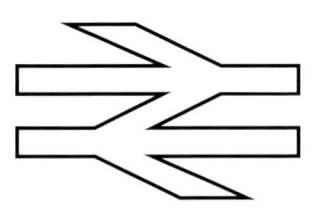

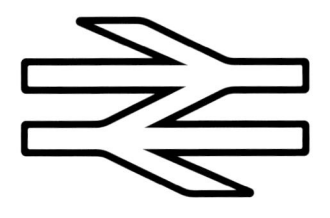

Having noted two different outline variants of the symbol, it is worth mentioning another dubious example which appeared in 1975 on the occasion of the launch of the High Speed Train (HST), which British Rail branded the Inter-City 125. The initial intention must have been to use an outline version of the symbol to match the specially drawn logotype **10.4**. It would become clear that an outline symbol lacked the required presence on the side of the power-car, so the inner contour was removed to leave a solid version of the symbol that would pack more of a punch. This failed to take into account that the finely tuned proportions of the symbol would be severely compromised; the resulting symbol was grossly overweight **10.5**. However it did not escape the attention of the Design Panel for long; a correctly drawn symbol **10.6** soon began to replace the corpulent interloper on HST power-cars.

10.4

10.5

10.6

10.7

10.8

10.9

10.10

British Rail activities were not wholly confined to the mainland; the organisation had a commercial arm that dealt with overseas travel and commerce. As such British Rail International was granted its own creative interpretation of the symbol 10.7, a patriotic remix of the Union Flag that went part way towards observing the arcane, vexillologically correct, thick and thin white strokes derived from the counterchanged and fimbriated saltires of Saint Andrew and Saint Patrick. The international symbol could also be used in the standard logotype format 10.8. No negative variant was made available on this occasion.

The concept itself was not brand new but had appeared as a motif for the celebrations of the 150th anniversary of the origin of passenger railways in 1975 10.9. The programme involved an exhibition train touring the country, a gala evening at the Royal Albert Hall and the official opening of the National Railway Museum.

James Cousins, Director of Industrial Design, was patently proud of this leftfield manifestation of the symbol and used it on the cover of his book *British Rail Design* 10.10, originally published by the Danish Design Council in 1986; a sumptuous publication that showcases the extensive design achievements of British Rail and documents some of the major challenges involved in implementing design policy across a large organisation.

This particular adaptation may not have been one for the design purists—it creates more visual problems than it solves—but it is difficult to deny its Britishness and thus its popular appeal; indeed it would not be the last time it was seen.

48

As British Rail rose to the huge challenge of applying its new image to all aspects of the business, a stencil version 10.11 became the means of standardising how the symbol should be applied in paint or ink to mark property such as tarpaulins, packing cases etc. The preferred colour for this application was Flame Red, although symbols of this ilk were sometimes stencilled in white onto red oxide freight wagons. It should be observed however that the structure of the symbol is such that it could quite satisfactorily be punched out of a solid sheet without the need for any struts at all. It therefore remains unclear why a boxed version was selected when a plain version would have yielded far more faithful results.

The last item in this section, a window sticker for travel agents 10.12, is included not so much for any notable divergence from the norm, although it was rare for a legend to be rendered in Publicity Blue, but rather for its design rationale 10.13, employing a 5:4 grid with a red 5:3 bounding box for the symbol; an uncharacteristic departure from the prescribed 8:5 proportion in the manual.

This straightforward, pared back approach typified the design philosophy embraced by British Rail, shunning all forms of self-indulgent extravagance or attention-seeking flourishes, preferring to distil design down to its purest form in order to avoid any dilution of the message. Even the unusual variants shown in this chapter maintain a commitment to clear communication and try to avoid confusion of any sort. If there had been a design mantra in the British Rail drawing office, it would surely have been: Keep it simple.

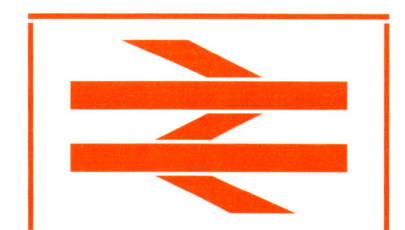

10.11

10.12

10.13

49

11
Significant outliers

As time went on and the British Rail corporate image became ingrained in the national psyche, the symbol was increasingly integrated into the branding devices of several subsidiaries, invariably to the detriment of the parent brand. This chapter explores a handful of examples where the forces of internal politics may have overridden or sidestepped the usual, sensible, design-driven decision-making process.

The Property Board logotype **11.1** designed in the early eighties comprised a ragtag cluster of silhouetted buildings—a reflection of the architectural diversity within the British Rail real estate portfolio—haphazardly thrown together to form an urban landscape above the standard symbol and legend. Internally dubbed the 'General Belgrano', an acerbic reference to the Argentine cruiser sunk by the British armed forces during the Falklands War in 1982, the nickname precisely dates its introduction and is a barometer of what staff thought of its design at the time.

British Rail Engineering Limited (known by the acronym BREL) was incorporated in 1969, amalgamating the activities of the former workshops division of British Rail with major production centres at Crewe, Derby, Doncaster, Glasgow, Shildon, Swindon and York. It would dawn upon some bright spark that the negative space to the left of the symbol could double as a letter 'E' of sorts and it was then only a matter of time before a crude 'B' and 'R' were being engineered and bolted on to create the lovably imperfect BREL logo **11.2**. A further variant **11.3** included an outline and the company name in full. But the BREL logo was not necessarily the work of genius that it purported to be.

Established in 1970, Golden Rail Holidays was British Rail's in-house package tour operator, offering short-break holidays, inclusive of hotels and transport, from one's local station to around 40 resorts in the United Kingdom and latterly to the Channel Islands and Continental Europe. The loss-making venture was renamed 'Gold Star Holidays' and eventually sold in May 1989 to the same company that had acquired British Transport Hotels in 1983. The original Golden Rail logo **11.4** was based upon eight British Rail symbols, arranged within an artisanal sun motif, the kind of thing that would not have looked out of place in *The Wicker Man*. Happily the arrangement was later toned down **11.5** but retained the banal repetition and rotation of the symbol, both of which were strictly forbidden in the guidelines and guaranteed to dilute the British Rail brand. The less said about the final iteration **11.6**, the better. Although the various Golden Rail logos make for an interesting and noteworthy addition to the British Rail brand portfolio, they do so on the basis of being salutary examples of how not to treat one's core brand. It is inconceivable to this author that the Design Panel would have been comfortable signing off projects that rode roughshod over their prized intellectual asset with such blatant disregard.

11.1 Property Board

11.2 BREL

11.3 BREL BRITISH RAIL ENGINEERING LIMITED

11.4

11.5 Golden Rail holidays

11.6 Golden Rail

51

11.8

11.9

Rail Riders provides a helpful illustration of the occasional need to integrate the British Rail symbol into a discrete operational entity with its own specific target audience and objectives. Founded by British Rail in 1981, the club offered discounted rail travel to junior enthusiasts aged 5–15 years, a quarterly magazine and free entry into Rail Riders World model railway at York.

The Rail Riders badge **11.8** incorporated the side-profile of the sleek and glamourous APT above the British Rail symbol. A similar circular pin badge—now a vintage collector's item—was included in the coveted membership pack. The popular association, which at its zenith boasted 80,000 members, even inspired Robin Wools, a West Yorkshire manufacturer of textile fibres, to release a knitting pattern for a sweater featuring the badge (see opposite).

The logo was updated in 1988 to reflect the changing British Rail traction scene **11.9**, the APT project having sadly fallen by the wayside in 1986. The treatment of the symbol was however altogether less respectful and the device all the poorer for it but that may not have prevented this particular space-aged atrocity from gaining cult status.

Rail Riders closed its doors in 1991 but, after nearly 30 years, the dormant brand was revived in 2020 by North Yorkshire promotional goods supplier Bufferbeam, now aiming the club at enthusiasts of all ages. The trademark was acquired by Simon Buxton and the original badge has been revived, along with memories of exotic excursions in punchy pullovers.

Knitting pattern for Rail Riders sweater by Robin Wools →
Gareth Peate

☐ A
☑ B
◉ C
☒ D
• E

12
Another dimension

Although British Rail made a concerted effort to ensure the symbol remained sacrosanct in its purest two-dimensional form, some signs—for example the station identifier at York **12.1**—were given depth to provide relief against various architectural backgrounds and the capacity for internal light fittings to make the illuminated symbol even more striking during the hours of darkness.

Eventually the temptation to introduce a three-dimensional variant in print would prove irresistible. A dynamic, attention-grabbing interpretation **12.2** first appeared on the cover of the British Rail passenger timetable in 1984 and was constructed using linear two-point perspective **12.3**. This device evolved further to incorporate five diverging passenger trains of various types into its composition and was used on the cover of the 1985 timetable **12.4**. As railway historian and broadcaster, Tim Dunn, commented on Twitter: "The British Rail passenger timetable of 1985 is what happened when an intern at the design studio watched too many Superman films and got a bit overexcited with a ruler." This static version was subsequently converted into a motion graphic for television advertising alongside J Walter Thompson's optimistic advertising slogan, *We're getting there*. A more convoluted and less effective variation on this theme **12.5** was later used in publicity for Rail Rover tickets.

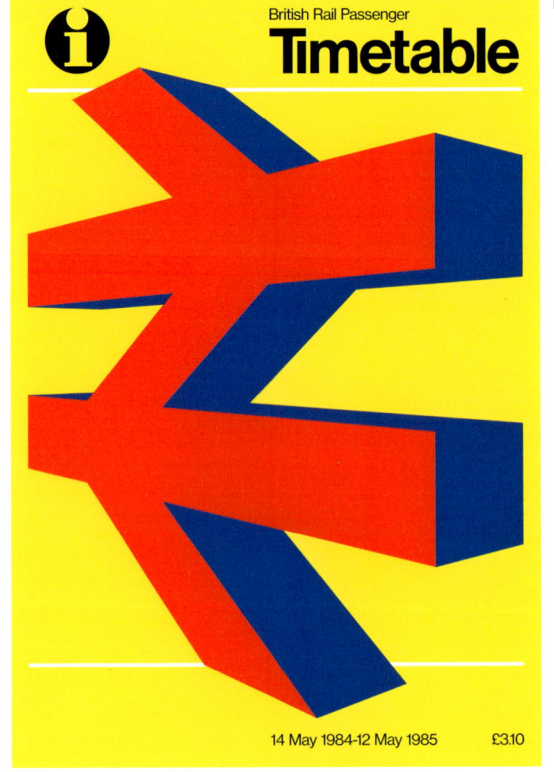

12.3

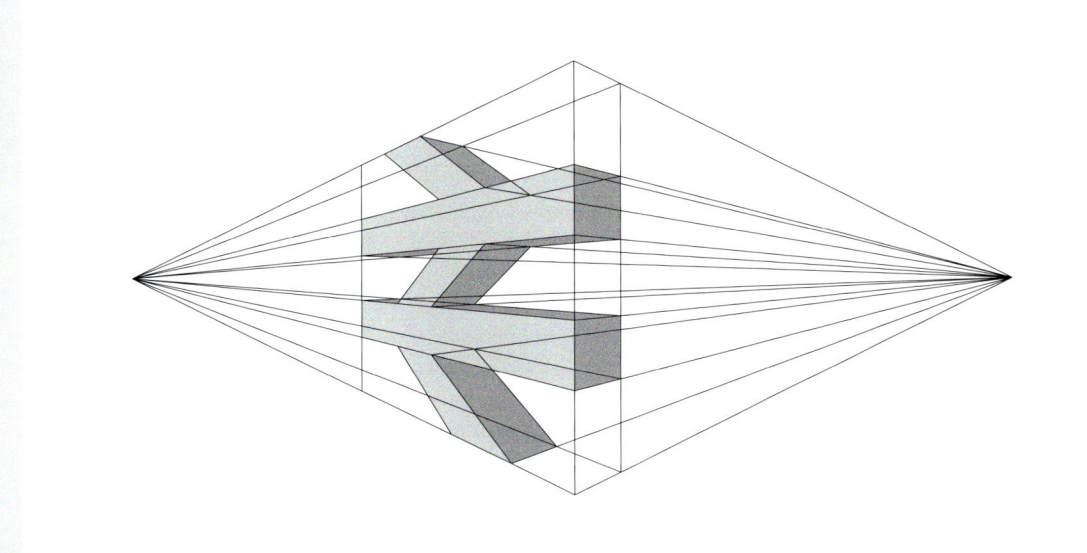

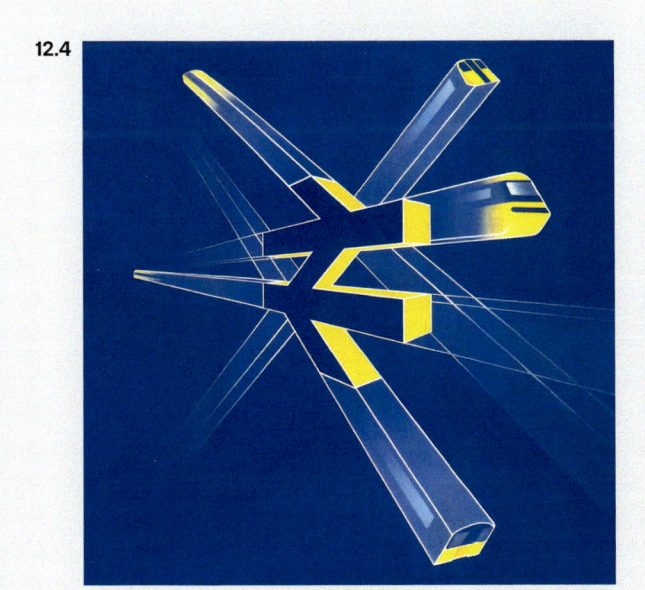

12.4

12.5

Tom Page

55

13
Sectorisation

Prior to restructuring in 1982, British Rail was organised into five regions, each responsible for the delivery of services within its own geography. On 1 January 1982, business operations were streamlined into separate commercial sectors in a bid to improve performance and increase profitability. Five new business sectors were formed: InterCity, London & South East, Provincial, Railfreight and Parcels. ScotRail would be added in 1983.

In branding terms, sectorisation flew in the face of the monolithic approach that British Rail had espoused for the best part of two decades, opening the door to a plethora of individual visual identities within the British Rail portfolio, each business eager to project its own distinct personality to its stakeholders. To begin with at least, the sectors observed time-honoured British Rail branding traditions, adhering to the prescribed logotype formula. There were also moves to embrace a more modern colour palette but, for a while at least, there broadly remained a family likeness across all sectors.

When it came to logos, the London & South East sector was first to try something a little different. Under the leadership of the influential Chris Green, a railwayman since 1965, Network SouthEast **13.1** was born on 10 June 1986. The identity was designed by Jordan Williams and featured a new livery, to replace the tasteful but arguably drab 'Jaffa cake' scheme, and its own branding device—the 'triple flash' **13.2**—which in certain situations was used in isolation of the British Rail symbol **13.3**.

InterCity and Railfreight both introduced bold, new identities in 1987. Railfreight turned to brand design consultancy Roundel Design to revitalise its public image. The solution was a radical departure from anything seen before at British Rail; a series of subsector symbols **13.4** that took their inspiration from the squadron markings of military aircraft. The expansive, unapologetic British Rail symbol used in the

13.4

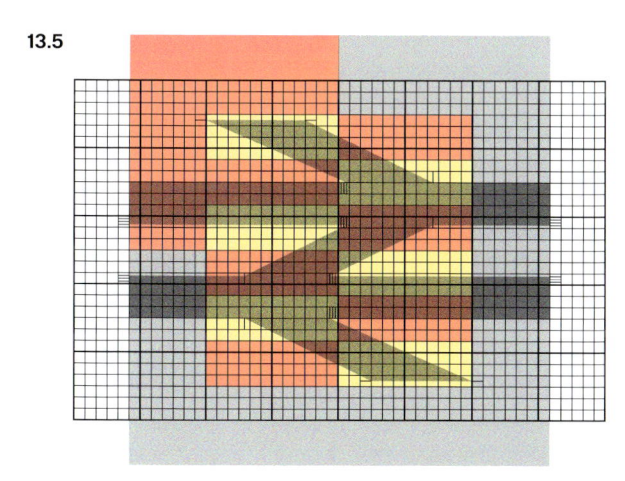

13.5

13.6

former Railfreight livery made way for elegant cast aluminium versions fitted discreetly below the cabside locomotive numbers (see overleaf). Whilst appearing to be otherwise unrelated, the proportions of the subsector symbols were derived from the eccentric geometry of the symbol **13.5**.

Meanwhile InterCity was financially faring well, becoming a profitable business under director John Prideaux, who engaged design consultants Newell and Sorrell to evolve the visual identity in readiness for the launch of the Class 91, the flagship locomotive built for the newly electrified East Coast Main Line. In contrast to Railfreight, InterCity chose to put more distance between itself and the British Rail symbol, purging it altogether from its livery and opting instead for a new swallow emblem accompanied by an InterCity logotype set in italic serif capitals **13.6**. Typographically it was about as far away from Rail Alphabet as could be and an indication that the symbol was no longer seen as the reliable force that it once was. Only in printed materials was the symbol retained, and even then as garnish, so to speak, where it had previously been the main course. The double arrow was beginning to fade.

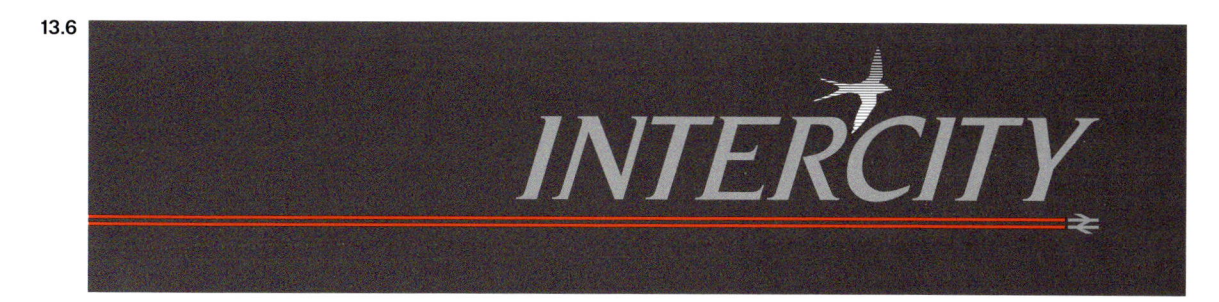

57

37688

Class 37/5 | X
Weight tonnes 107

Visual differentiation gathered pace into the nineties as a prelude to the privatisation of British Rail by John Major's Conservative government. Next to receive a facelift was the loss-making Provincial sector. Lloyd Northover provided the new look, which was unveiled in late 1990. Although the familiar Provincial blues were retained, a couple of muted greys were added to the colour palette. Notably there was a new name for the sector that had effectively become a dumping ground for all passenger services that did not fit neatly into either InterCity or Network SouthEast. The Regional Railways logotype **13.7** was set in a modified version of Eric Gill's Joanna typeface to provide a measure of sophistication for the brand and a diminutive British Rail symbol appeared as an endorsement. ScotRail was afforded matching treatment **13.8**.

Following the success of the popular new Railfreight scheme, Roundel Design were again approached to bring their bold, refreshing perspective to the Parcels sector. Launched in October 1991, Rail express systems (R.e.s.) adopted a mythological 'winged plus' **13.9**. The use of the British Rail symbol was however limited solely to locomotives, an understated, if not apologetic, mark of asset ownership.

In the lead-up up to privatisation, the British Rail symbol, once the undisputed star of the show, no longer retained top billing but had evidently been relegated to little more than an afterthought, at best a concession, shoe-horned into several disparate and otherwise unrelated sub-brands, a seal guaranteeing the provenance of the various constituents being geared up for sale to the highest bidder.

13.7

13.8

13.9

← Cast aluminium alloy British Rail symbol applied to a Class 37 locomotive

Stockport

14
Local self-expression

As with any large, national organisation, there will always be the significant temptation for regional and local visual differentiation; an individualism fuelled by a heady mixture of misplaced provincial or departmental pride, a strong sense of self-importance or the need to matter, a justifiable desire to boost morale or a reluctance to embrace the authority of a head office thought to be so far removed as to be completely out of touch with the operations of a neglected workforce out in the field.

In the case of the railways, which for many years had enjoyed devolved management and thus relative autonomy at regional level, in addition to what was deemed to be a healthy level of competition between different routes that had previously vied for custom, it is perhaps not surprising that the reflex of the business was often to look inwards in a quest to find itself in an age of cold, characterless, business-wide brand edicts. Nevertheless unrestrained, parochial self-expression is the enemy of monolithic corporate identity and this led to a number of heinous branding crimes.

It is well-attested that the people of Cornwall have long thought of themselves as a nation in their own right, quite independent from the rest of Britain: Cornish station announcers have been known to blame late-running services upon points failures and the like 'up in England'. Little wonder that Kernow made a statement of intent with the creation of its own sub-brand, an initiative that appears to have been positively encouraged by British Rail Western Region management to lift industry spirits in the Duchy. Conceived in 1983, Cornish Railways was the brainchild of Rusty Eplett, a charismatic Truro railwayman who did much to promote the local railways at that time. Eplett introduced two visual devices: The first was a crest consisting of two crossed flags—British Rail and St Piran—below the county shield. The second was the winning entry in a competition to design a new mascot for Cornish Railways—a cartoon lizard nicknamed 'Wizzy', draped casually around a red British Rail symbol **14.1**. It is thought that only three Class 37 locomotives allocated to St Blazey depot (37181, 37185 and 37207) were thus emblazoned before Head Office got wind of the branding deviance and promptly ordered its removal. Whether or not the removal of a layer of rail management in Cornwall was necessary to achieve this end remains unclear.

← Textured sheet steel station identifier at Stockport

14.2

Even further from the corridors of power in 222 Marylebone Road, the railways of the far north, whose regional headquarters were in Inverness, were subjected in 1984 to a similarly ill-conceived motif **14.2**, taking as its inspiration the much admired *Monarch of the Glen*, painted in 1851 by Sir Edwin Landseer, depicting a resplendent red deer stag against the backdrop of dark and threatening skies over a rugged and imposing Scottish wilderness. The painting was originally commissioned to hang in the Palace of Westminster but since 2017 it has proudly been a part of the collection at the Scottish National Gallery in Edinburgh. The name Highland Rail was a throwback to the Highland Railway, one of the smaller British railways before the Railways Act 1921. The Highland Rail stag logo, beloved of enthusiasts and modellers alike, relegated the British Rail symbol to the very bottom and was applied to the fleet of locomotives allocated to Inverness. The motif also appeared in isolation on station and depot signage in the Highlands.

As seen in the previous chapter, in the early eighties British Rail restructured its operations into distinct business sectors, the majority of which (for example, InterCity and Railfreight) were organised according to the particular service offered. However some sectors retained a geographical focus, like ScotRail, which provided passenger services within the Scottish Region. Chris Green was appointed its general manager in 1984 and tasked with rolling out the identity which had only just been introduced in late 1983; it was not long before the unique light blue ScotRail brand had been applied across the board north of the border. Although the British Rail Corporate Identity adequately catered for a ScotRail sub-brand in the form of a standard British Rail logotype arrangement **14.3**, that did not prevent the emergence of a suspect, unofficial variant, consisting of a combination of a badly drawn British Rail symbol and a stylised silhouette of mainland Scotland **14.4**. This logo was used to promote the reopening of the Bathgate Link in March 1986, even appearing on some of the rolling stock used on the route. That this variant was short-lived and rarely seen would suggest that the British Rail Design Panel were not especially enamoured by it, not least because of its lamentable lack of respect for the British Rail symbol, not to mention the hard outline of Scotland with the inevitable absence of a multitude of islands that representations of this nature are in the habit of omitting.

British Rail adopted the Robin Hood Line name and logotype **14.5** for the 1993 reopening of the line from Nottingham to Newstead, a relative latecomer to the British Rail network. Introduced at a time when much of the industry was preparing for privatisation, the line was later extended to Mansfield, which hitherto had become the largest town in England to have been deprived of a station following the closure of the passenger service in October 1964. Today the line extends as far north as Worksop. In an ultimately disdainful treatment of the British Rail symbol, the logo features two adjoining arrows in [Lincoln?] green with yellow fletching, plucked, one assumes, from the fulsome quiver of the eponymous legend, hero and outlaw of nearby Sherwood Forest. It is difficult to know how a 'designer' could so nonchalantly have taken an unholy scalpel to such a sacred artefact and still manage to sleep soundly at night. One can only imagine this logo was the stuff of establishment nightmares, not unlike Robin Hood himself.

While this chapter is in no way intended to be an exhaustive record of the sort of use and abuse that the British Rail symbol routinely had to endure, often in the hands of wayward local managers, it serves to provide clear evidence that this kind of initiative rarely, if ever, has anything of substance to add to a master-brand apart from rustic quaintness and confused messaging, neither of which satisfactorily serve a single, overarching brand strategy. It is nevertheless instructive for the student of design to include a hall of shame like this, no matter how retina-searingly painful encounters with such initiatives are bound to become.

14.3

14.4

14.5

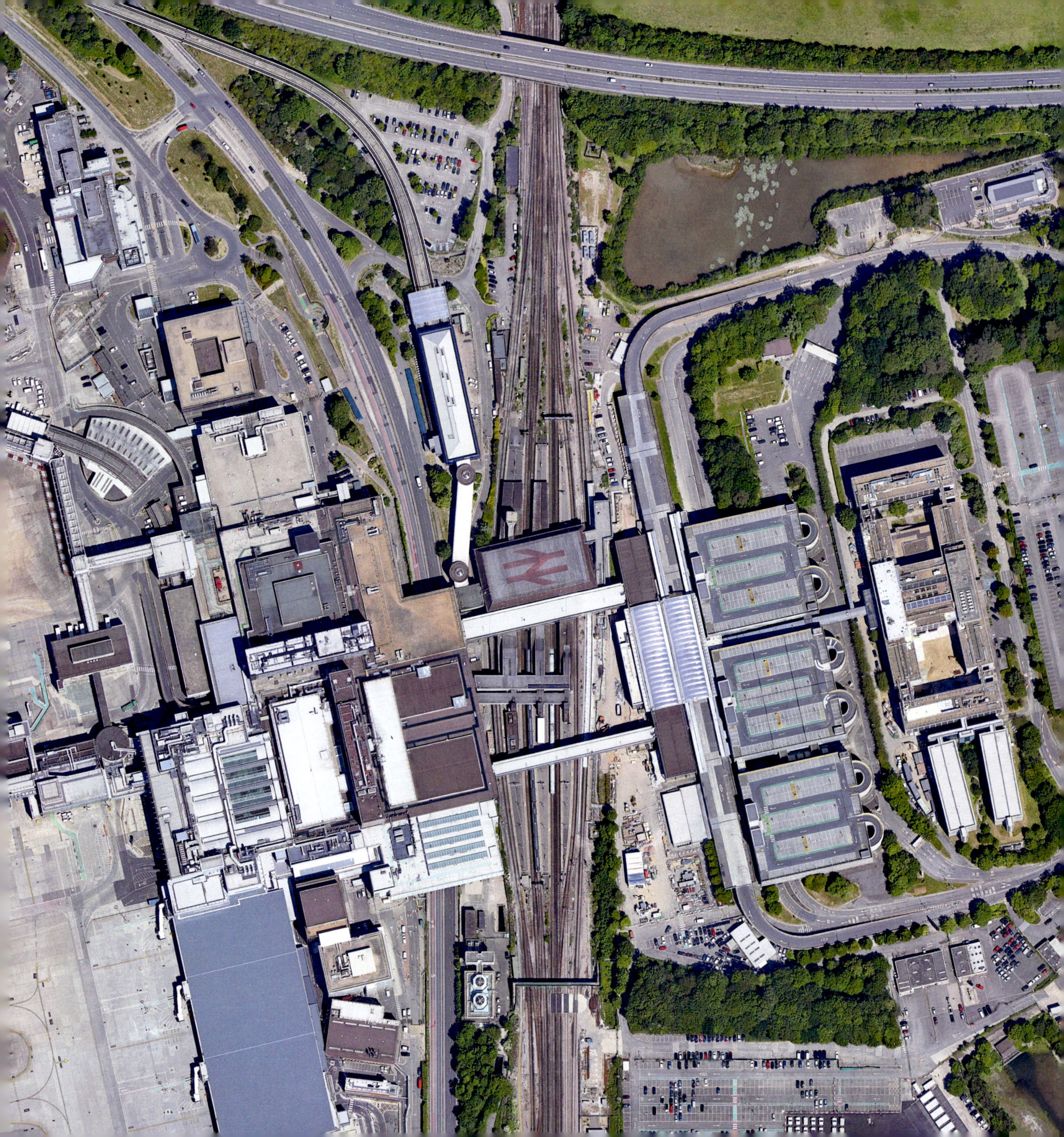

15
Size matters

The largest British Rail symbol used as a station identifier is thought to be situated in the atrium at Milton Keynes Central **15.1**. The super-sized symbol has been there since the station was opened in 1982, a fitting treatment at the focal point of the vast mirrored glass edifice, which doubled as the headquarters of the United Nations in the 1987 film *Superman IV: The Quest For Peace*, for which the symbol was shrouded in dark fabric.

However the award for the largest symbol in existence must go to the colossus that adorns the flat roof of the station concourse at Gatwick Airport **15.2**. The symbol has an x-height of 12m, making the whole thing a staggering 38m wide, easily visible from landing aircraft.

When it comes to the smallest British Rail symbol to have been reproduced, it would be hard to beat the version used on a Royal Mail postage stamp commemorating Harry Beck's London Underground map **15.3**. Issued as part of the British Design Classics series in January 2009, the stamp, designed by London creative consultancy HGV, depicts Zone 1, the central area of the Underground. The symbol is used on tube maps to indicate National Rail services. Although the Corporate Identity Manual allowed for the symbol to be printed an eighth of an inch (3.175mm) wide, the width of the minuscule symbol in this instance is estimated to be less than half a millimetre.

15.1
@diamondgeezer

15.2
Network Rail

15.3

← Aerial view of Gatwick Airport
Imagery ©2024 Bluesky, Infoterra Ltd & Bluesky, Maxar Technologies/Map data ©2024 Google

16
Low fidelity

Sooner or later, the question would be asked: 'What happens when the British Rail symbol is reproduced in low resolution?' Unfortunately the answer was invariably negative. However if something is generally considered a bad idea, this will in no way deter either the ignorant or foolhardy from giving it a shot and embarking on a journey that is likely to end in tears.

Designed in a strictly analogue era, the predominantly angular nature of the British Rail symbol, having six oblique edges, does nothing but roundly mock the straightjacket of the computer screen or any other similar rectilinear grid that attempts to entertain any such ill-advised application.

Such was the case in the realm of teletext, a former standard for displaying basic text and graphics on suitably equipped television sets, which not every reader may recall. The ultra-restrictive, rasterised 3-bit universe afforded only eight basic RGB colour permutations and was not remotely conducive to displaying graphics satisfactorily and many gratuitously 'blocky' design offences were committed.

The British Rail symbol first appeared on Oracle, ITV's proprietary teletext service, in the early eighties, where British Rail travel bulletins could be found fittingly on page 125. In what must surely be considered one of its most unfortunate manifestations to date, the symbol would barely have been recognisable were it not for the equally poorly rendered British Rail name alongside it **16.1**. An irksome arrangement in which every third horizontal row of pixels was half as tall again further suggests that, in yielding to the limitations of this rudimentary technology, the device had been hard-fitted to a most inconvenient grid **16.2**, the net result being an abysmal representation of the symbol, the like of which may not have been witnessed before or since, although it is with considerable apprehension that this claim is made.

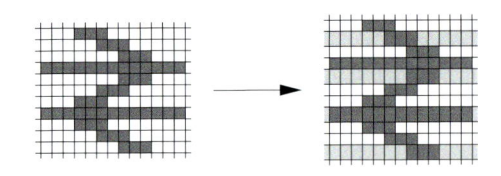

16.3

British Transport Films/Science Museum Group

16.4

British Transport Films/Science Museum Group

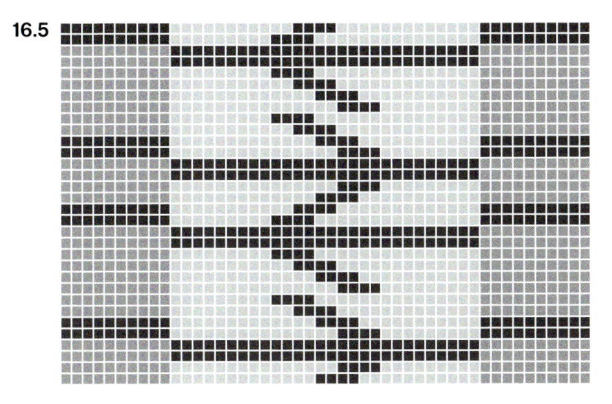

In the earliest days of the British Rail brand, a slightly more successful attempt had been made to apply the symbol to a fixed grid in the form of a repeating pattern for the corporate carpet, albeit flagrantly ignoring the sage advice that the prospect of walking all over one's brand should never be entertained. In the interests of equality, two similar photographs— 'his' **16.3** and 'hers' **16.4**—were produced by British Rail for marketing purposes; it was a different age! The symbol itself was adjusted to fit a 28 × 16 grid **16.5** and repeated on alternating light and dark colour bands. These evocative photographs have become part of British Rail folklore but the symbol itself is lightweight and underwhelming and does scant justice to the original. Using a 32 × 20 (8:5) grid would have yielded better results **16.6**, giving the symbol an increased presence with far greater fidelity to the original design, although the parameters of the carpet manufacturing process in question may have precluded such an approach.

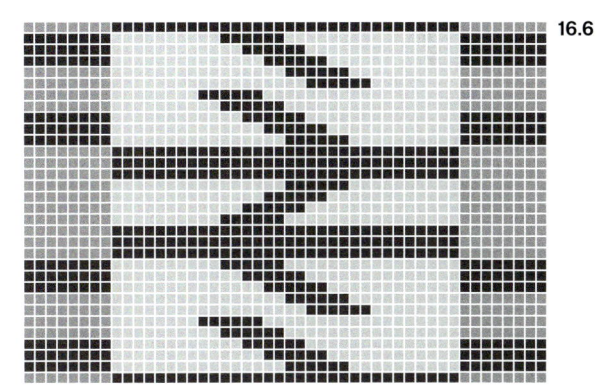

16.5

16.6

67

16.7

The British Rail symbol can sometimes be seen on information displays on the platforms of the Underground. LEDs arranged in a dot matrix format, in either the 1 or 0 state, i.e. on or off, can be formed into plain text and have the useful capability of scrolling across the display to allow for a greater amount of data within the fixed space. The same fundamental question once again arises: How should the symbol be rendered in a finite grid of very few elements with minimum compromise?

The example above **16.7**, taken from a next train indicator on the Edgware branch of the Northern Line, which in this case fills a 9 × 7 space, does not bear close scrutiny, although when viewed from a distance it could be said to do a job of sorts. The glaring lack of rotational symmetry is a concern and gives the symbol an unnerving, lop-sided appearance **16.8**.

In the information age, the performance of any logo within the constraints of the digital environment has become a key consideration in brand design. Producing a decent logo at a low resolution can cause major headaches.

The favicon—the tiny image that appears in the address bar of web browsers—has an extremely limited canvas (originally just 16 × 16 pixels), which presents unique rendering challenges. This point is well illustrated by the *nationalrail.co.uk* favicon **16.9**. Even at 48 × 48 pixels, the symbol is creaking. Additionally an even distribution of the pixels depends upon the symbol being centred on the available area, which is clearly not the case here.

With such emphasis now placed on digital, one wonders whether the British Rail symbol may have looked substantially different had it been designed in the twenty-first century?

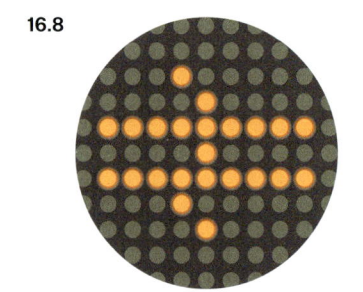

16.8

16.9

Digital symbol displayed on a First Bus service in Bath →

City Centre 5
FREE
WiFi
MUST BE WORN
69457
69457
Bath city
WX59 BZL

Station

17
One for the road

When the Ministry of Transport (now the Department for Transport) prescribed the British Rail symbol to represent railway stations on Kinneir and Calvert's celebrated UK traffic signs, the proportions of the symbol were adjusted to accommodate the principle of using 'stroke width'—notionally a quarter of the lower-case x-height—to specify all dimensions for sign layouts **17.1**.

Although the symbol always appears in a negative format on traffic signs, it is in fact significantly heavier than the original negative version and, whilst the red box faithfully retains its 8:5 ratio, the ratio of the symbol itself has been modified to 5:3 (as opposed to the standard 38:23 which understandably is not conducive to the stroke width system).

The overall height of the two horizontal tracks of the symbol still directly relates to the x-height of the accompanying legend but in the traffic signs layout, in contrast to the alignment conventions of Rail Alphabet, the symbol does not vertically align to the lower-case x-height, which is generally lowered by 0.5 sw (half a stroke width), theoretically to give improved typographic balance to signs **17.2**.

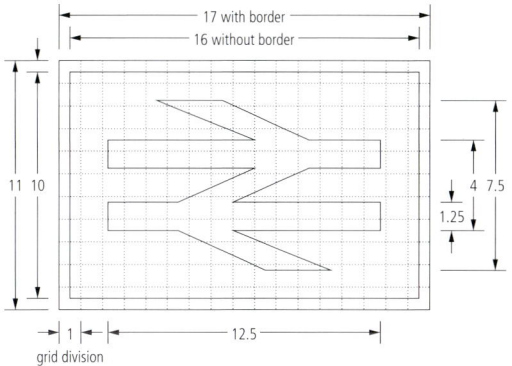

← Traffic sign in Sheffield city centre

18
Civic duty

The fabulously peculiar domain of civic heraldry throws up a wealth of fascinating associations in the arms of many municipal organisations. However there is only one known occasion when the British Rail symbol has crossed the threshold into this medium.

Founded on 1 April 1974, the Metropolitan Borough of Doncaster was officially granted its coat of arms by the College of Arms in 1975. So synonymous had the South Yorkshire town become with the railway industry that the British Rail symbol was included in its arms.

The full-colour coat of arms displayed in relief above the entrance of Doncaster's tourist information office **18.1** is, like most civic armorial bearings, an object of great poise and artistic beauty. The dexter (right) supporter—the beast to the left of the arms from an onlooker's point of view—is formally described in heraldic terms thus: 'On the dexter side a Lion sejant Or that on the dexter gorged with a representation of the device of British Rail Gules pendent therefrom a Miner's Safety Lamp proper.'

This original coat of arms was digitised, with fairly rudimentary autotrace technology, having minimal attention paid to the British Rail collar, which has been disfigured almost beyond recognition. A striking stainless steel fabrication of those arms **18.2** is displayed prominently on the facade of the Civic Offices.

18.3

Doncaster Council

18.4

BE STEADFAST

18.5

The borough invested in a visual identity refresh in 2017, becoming known simply as Doncaster Council **18.3**. The coat of arms was reimagined by graphic artist and illustrator Albert Morell on behalf of Barnsley branding agency Ledgard Jepson **18.4**.

Close inspection of the new arms shows a much improved British Rail symbol **18.5**, albeit drawn with parallel arms, truncated on the left and tilted at a jaunty 25° angle. A simplified mining lantern is casually slung over the lower arm, where it had previously hung over one of the symbol's horizontal tracks; the lamp would be certain to fall to the ground were this not an imaginary scenario where the laws of physics can be conveniently suspended in the name of heraldic creativity.

More than 150 years after the first steam locomotive proudly rolled off the shop floor at Doncaster, there is sadly no longer the appetite for British-built trains that there once was. Engineering at the Works has been in steady decline since the site was broken up in 1987 as British Rail revisited its manufacturing and maintenance policy. The main locomotive repair shop on the Crimpsall was sold to a developer in 2004 and later demolished to make way for new housing.

Awarded city status as part of HM Queen Elizabeth II's Platinum Jubilee celebrations in 2022, Doncaster will forever be the place that brought us Nigel Gresley's *Flying Scotsman* and *Mallard*. In the meantime a fearsome, mythical lion with a lop-sided logo for a collar continues to serve as a reminder of the city's important, influential and illustrious railway heritage.

73

19
Up, up and away

In May 1984 British Rail launched Gatwick Express, a dedicated 30-minute shuttle service linking London Victoria and Gatwick Airport, with departures every 15 minutes by day and hourly throughout the night. The memorable promotional campaign created by fledgling advertising agency Hedger Mitchell Stark featured a playful treatment of the British Rail symbol where the upper portion of the device was daringly detached and slanted to simulate a plane taking off **19.1**.

    Chiltern Railways provided a more recent example of the dissection of the symbol in the name of humour as part of their Summer 2018 *Travel Free Range* campaign, produced by creative and media agency The Gate London. Taking little more than half of the symbol, just as the Gatwick Express poster had so craftily done all those years ago, the resulting shape was repeated to suggest the footprints of a chicken, enjoying the freedom to roam the network to its heart's content **19.2**.

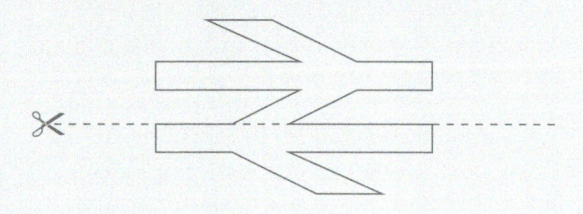

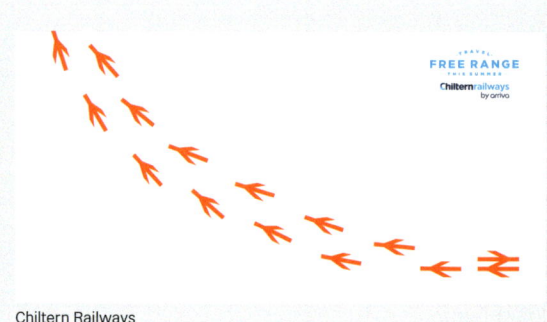

19.1

GATWICK EXPRESS.
CATCH THE TRAIN AND YOU'VE CAUGHT THE PLANE.

19.2

Chiltern Railways

74

Two-part composite symbol at Worcestershire Parkway →

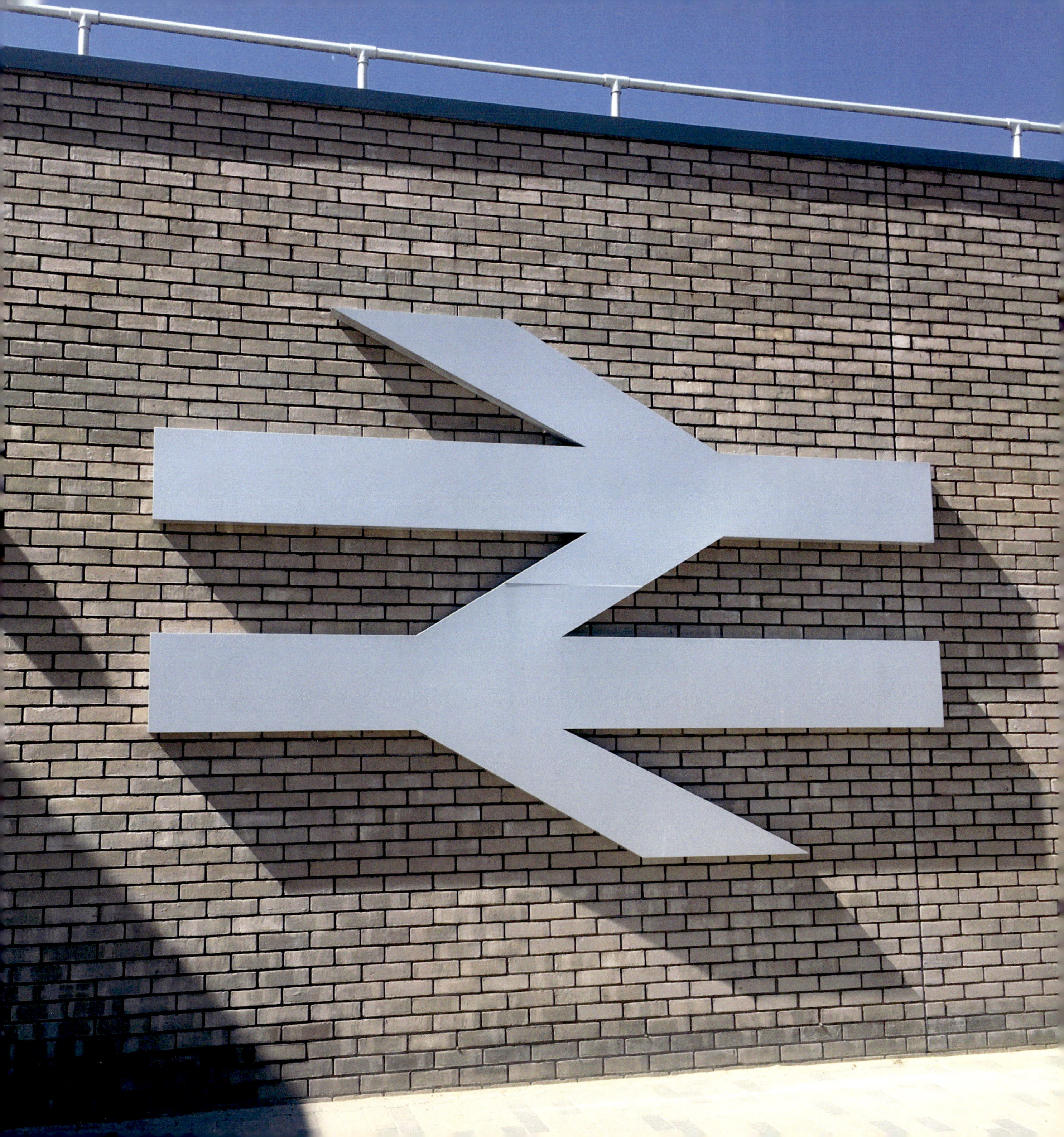

20
Artistic licence

Occasions where the British Rail symbol has been incorporated into the architecture of the railways are plentiful and diverse, many falling under the broad category of art.

The building or refurbishment of a railway station provides the scope to explore creative brand expression in unique ways. The brutalist fountain at the eastern end of the forecourt of the redeveloped London Euston **20.1** raised more than a few eyebrows at the time of its installation in 1968. The earlier demolition of the Euston Arch, a Doric propylaeum built in 1837, remains to some a mindless act of vandalism, exacerbated by what was to replace it. At the time of writing, this once imposing concrete column could hardly be seen, engulfed on all sides by a cluster of fast food outlets.

Composition of the symbol from tiles or tesserae presents challenges around how the angular arms of the symbol will be rendered. In the multi-tiled digital clock tower at Hackney Central **20.2**—overclad in white since the station transferred to TfL Overground in 2007—the artist chose to curtail the horizontal strokes of the symbol at the same oblique angle as the sides of the structure itself.

Badry Mostafa's colourful 1983 mural design at King's Cross Thameslink **20.3**, the winner of a competition run by British Rail and London Transport, features an imaginative interlocking of the British Rail symbol and Edward Johnston's Underground roundel. Whether it can be said to have done justice to the brand assets of either organisation is moot.

The wrought, galvanised steel railings at Haymarket station in Edinburgh **20.4** fitted during its reconstruction in 2012 provide an engaging optical effect from multiple angles, adding some welcome visual interest to what might otherwise be just another grey and soulless platform.

20.1

Chris Timings/Design Research Unit

20.2

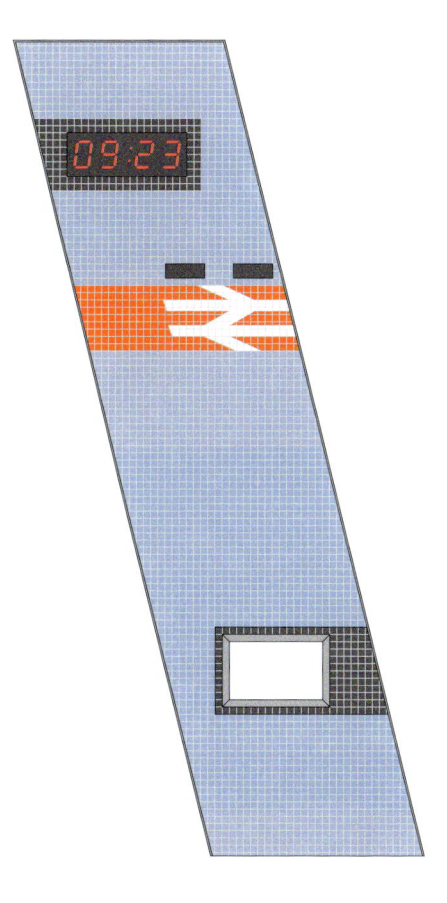

20.3

Tim Dunn

20.4

Luke Davydaitis

20.5

Ben Sutherland

Pushing the British Rail Corporate Identity to its limits, the cunningly conceived four-way totem at Sevenoaks **20.5** overlooked the station environs for many years until its removal during refurbishment in 2012. The difficult decision to dismantle the sign may have had something to do with the local pigeons and their associated activities. It is a sad loss nonetheless and one can only hope that the magnificent item found a loving home and a deserving clean-up.

21
Look back in anger

Founded in 2009 by Glasgow-based artist and activist Ellie Harrison, Bring Back British Rail describes itself as 'the collective voice of disgruntled rail passengers and disheartened train employees, demanding a re-unified national rail network run for people not profit'. Its instantly recognisable logo, designed by Fraser Muggeridge, features a mirror image of the British Rail symbol **21.1**.

As calls have grown for Britain's railways to be renationalised, evidence of the persistent activities of the pressure group has spread far and wide **21.2**. The powerful British Rail imagery has also been used by campaigners to great effect at various public demonstrations **21.3**.

A series of four placards **21.4**, based on an original design concept by UHC (Ultimate Holding Company)—a Manchester-based co-operative social enterprise working alongside ethically motivated organisations and campaigns—uses the mirrored symbol as a repeating watermark along with a pastiche of the trademark page numbering style **21.5** taken from the British Rail Corporate Identity Manual.

This must be the first time that the British Rail symbol has been intentionally mirrored since its application to the funnels of British Rail ships. And since no-one appears to be ultimately responsible for regulating usage of the symbol, this daring improvisation remains largely unchallenged.

Ellie Harrison

Robin Prime

21.4

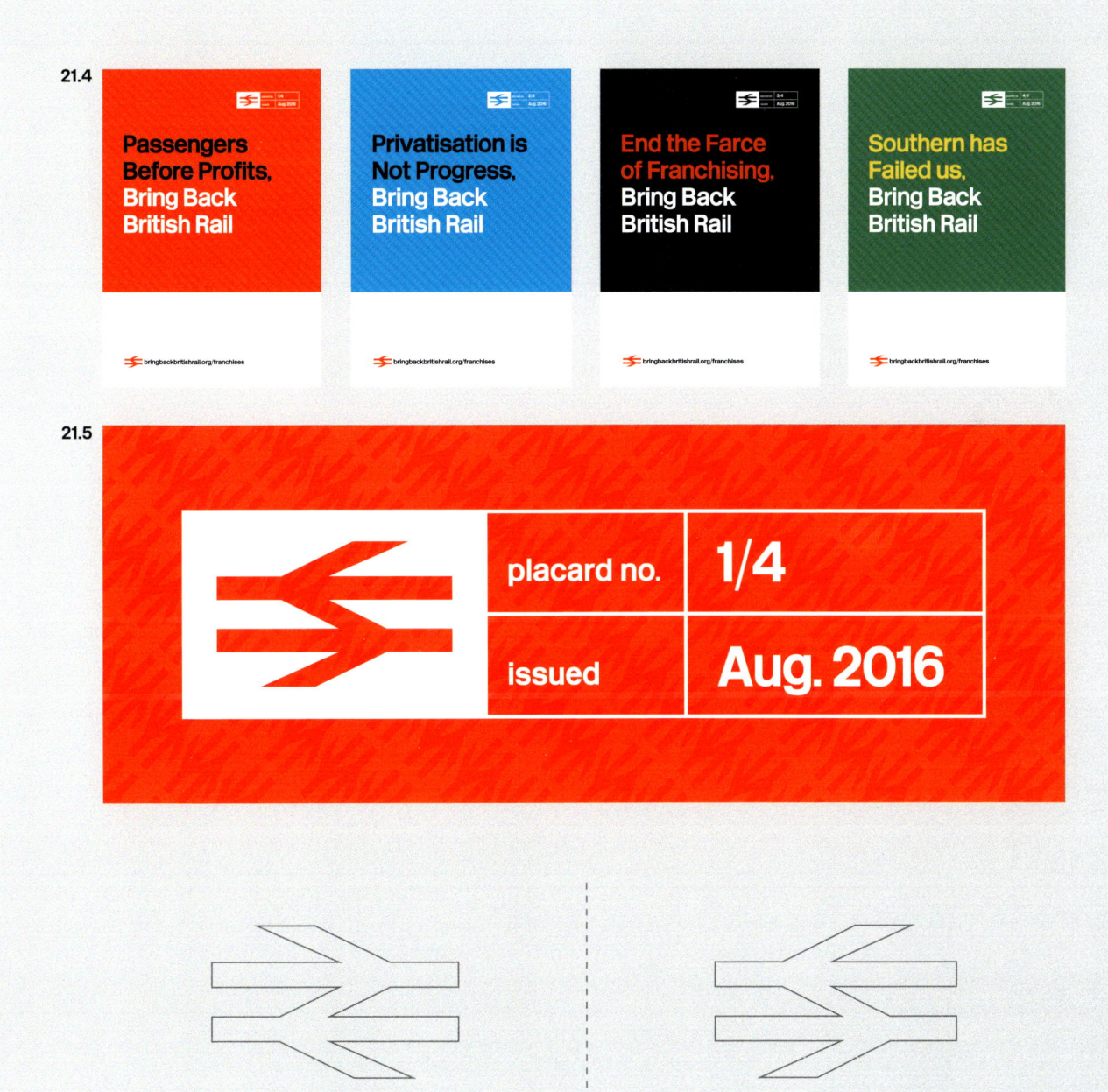

Passengers Before Profits, **Bring Back British Rail**

Privatisation is Not Progress, **Bring Back British Rail**

End the Farce of Franchising, **Bring Back British Rail**

Southern has Failed us, **Bring Back British Rail**

bringbackbritishrail.org/franchises

21.5

| placard no. | 1/4 |
| issued | Aug. 2016 |

22
The privatisation era

In this digital age, logos—even rather good ones—come and go as a matter of course. However the timeless British Rail symbol simply will not be shown the door but has demonstrably answered any critics it may once have had by far outlasting the company that it once so proudly represented. Today the double arrow retains its significant design stature and remains an inspirational concept that continues to encapsulate the railways perfectly.

The Railways Act 1993, passed by John Major's Conservative government, led to the restructuring of British Rail and the effective privatisation of the railways. Recognising the inherent value in the symbol, the Department for Transport sensibly held on tightly to the intellectual property, which faithfully continues to serve the railway industry and the nation, still appearing on paper tickets **22.1** and signage to identify National Rail stations and services.

The National Rail trade name is licensed by the Rail Delivery Group to train operating companies in England, Scotland and Wales. The logotype **22.2** comprises a roundel containing the symbol coupled with text in modified Sassoon Bold, a typeface family designed for teaching reading and handwriting. One could be forgiven for thinking that the guardians of the symbol would take good care of it, yet close scrutiny of their own artwork reveals a slight compression of the symbol **22.3**. Furthermore

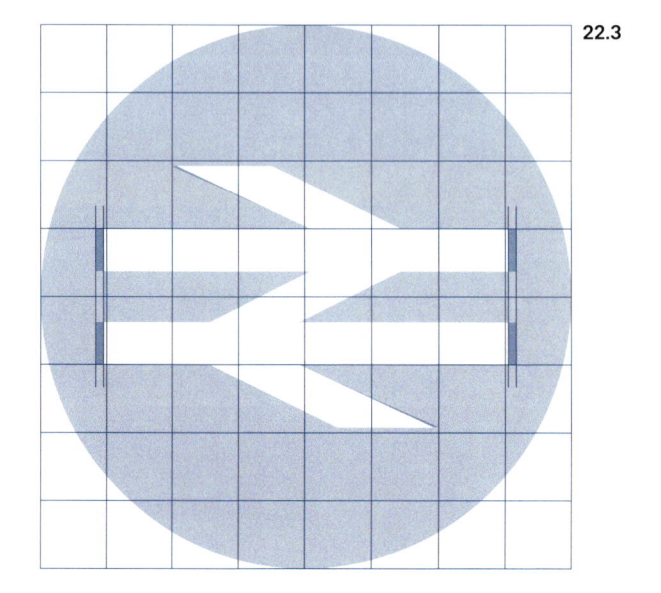

80

22.4

22.5

22.6

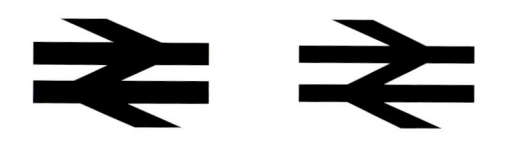

National Rail's very own brand usage guidelines somehow contrived to mix up the positive and negative symbols, explaining: 'It is important to know that the reversed version is not just a white copy of the positive version. It is actually slightly heavier [sic] in weight to give the visual impression of being the same when reversed.' Precisely the opposite is true!

If the brand custodians are unclear about how the symbol should be reproduced, it will come as no surprise to find train operating companies routinely playing fast and loose with the symbol across the network. With little or no desire to turn this section into a rogue's gallery, attention will be focused on just one notable example where the symbol has derailed: First noted as a replacement vinyl applied over an original sun-bleached symbol at Chelford **22.4**, this gross impostor—dubbed 'the Chonk' by railway engineer and writer, Gareth Dennis— was propagated in error, following its upload to a rail industry database. It can now be found 'adorning' many stations across northern England and Wales, such as Alderley Edge **22.5**. In addition to a visual comparison with the correct version of the symbol **22.6**, no further comment on its shortcomings is required.

Under privatisation the integrity of the symbol remains under greater threat than at any point in its proud history. It is very difficult to see how matters can be improved while responsibility for its consistent application falls between different stalls with no demonstrable desire or incentive to get it right.

81

There came another twist in 2016; London advertising and communications agency M&C Saatchi came up with the *Britain Runs on Rail* campaign for the Rail Delivery Group, the organisation that represents the owners of Britain's passenger and freight operators, HS2 and Network Rail. The purpose of the innovative campaign was to highlight the crucial role the national railway industry plays in Britain's economy and to inform the public about the ongoing improvements across the country's railway network.

The campaign logo **22.7** generated much interest at its launch in September 2016, due in part to its creative reinterpretation of the British Rail symbol, not only for its five vivid colours, representing many railway companies working closely together—the original symbol was of course designed specifically for single colour usage—but also for the abject distortion of the device itself with its grotesquely long arms, which severely disturb the equilibrium of the original mark.

Gerry Barney, designer of the original symbol, is said to have welcomed the refreshed version, praising it as "a faithful adaptation of my original 1965 design" although one cannot help but wonder what he really made of the grim alteration. Whether he actually clapped eyes on M&C Saatchi's version of the logo remains a matter of conjecture.

This technicolour symbol more recently plied its trade as the basis of the Rail Delivery Group initiative *Big Plans. Big Changes.* **22.8** to deliver a more customer-focused, joined-up and accountable railway in the United Kingdom. For this manifestation, the garish combination of discordant hues were retained but thankfully the device had reverted to more familiar and acceptable proportions. It was a considerable improvement on its long-armed antecedent and an admission of sorts that the previous incarnation was an ill-judged and inadvisable departure from the original design aesthetic, at least where the geometry is concerned, if not the bizarre colour scheme.

However there appears to have been no subsequent loss of appetite for dividing of the

22.7

22.8

22.9

22.10

symbol up into various blocks of colour. In September 2021, the Rail Delivery Group launched its *We Mean Green* campaign to encourage more people to take the train and more businesses to consider rail freight. The objective was to build awareness that rail is easily the greenest form of public transport, one that will need to play its part if the UK is to achieve any future net-zero carbon goal.

The agency behind the campaign, Studio Blackburn, made an ill-advised return to M&C Saatchi's long-armed symbol, this time daubing it in five shades of green **22.9**. On this occasion, Gerry Barney was rather more forthright in his opinions. In an interview with the Guardian, Barney said, "I think that's rubbish. I could understand it if they had just swapped red for green. But why on earth have they got that many colours? It's a load of old bollocks. It's just a mess." Who can say with any certainty why Barney's diatribe against this green eyesore appears to run counter to the quote with which he was attributed when the psychedelic symbol first appeared in 2016?

To draw this depressing chapter to a close, in the wake of what has effectively been a case study in how *not* to manage the most valuable of branding assets, there is conveniently just enough space to mention one final aberration **22.10** which first appeared in 2021 as a means of encouraging passengers back onto the railway after 18 months of the brutal and unforgiving COVID-19 pandemic. Opaquely described by the Rail Delivery Group as a 'TOC [train operating company] alignment device' as part of the Rail Recovery Marketing Campaign, the symbol was fattened up to accommodate a two-line slogan within its horizontals, aimed at convincing the nation that a return to rail travel was the way to embrace a brighter, post-pestilence future. A further iteration with a watered-down message did precisely nothing to mask the bewildering lack of appreciation for the integrity of symbol.

In recent years Gerry Barney's brilliant British Rail symbol has fallen on hard times. After so many years of steadfast service, it surely deserves far better. This saddened me but also got me thinking…

83

23
What if?

As a fully paid-up member of the DRU school of rational design theory and a long-time adherent to the basic tenets of modernism, it seemed churlish, disloyal, treacherous even, to entertain thoughts of how the British Rail symbol might be improved in any way. Surely Gerry Barney had totally nailed it all those years ago as he made his prodigious scribbles on the tube? Nevertheless, throughout the compilation of this book, the nagging question 'What if?' would surface time and again. While the manifold virtues of the original symbol have been thoroughly—even pathologically—extolled in the preceding chapters, perhaps there still remained some room for improvement? And so began a cautious dissection and reworking of the symbol in a quest to iron out any creases with a view to locking it down once and for all, future-proofing it for generations to come.

Whilst the theoretical intention of DRU to guarantee consistency of appearance across British Rail by specifying two versions of the symbol may reasonably have been considered praiseworthy at first glance, too often the reality at ground level was different. Use of the wrong optical variant became a predictably common mistake, which suggests—with the considerable benefit of hindsight—that such lofty idealism ought to have yielded at the outset to more measured and less ambitious pragmatism.

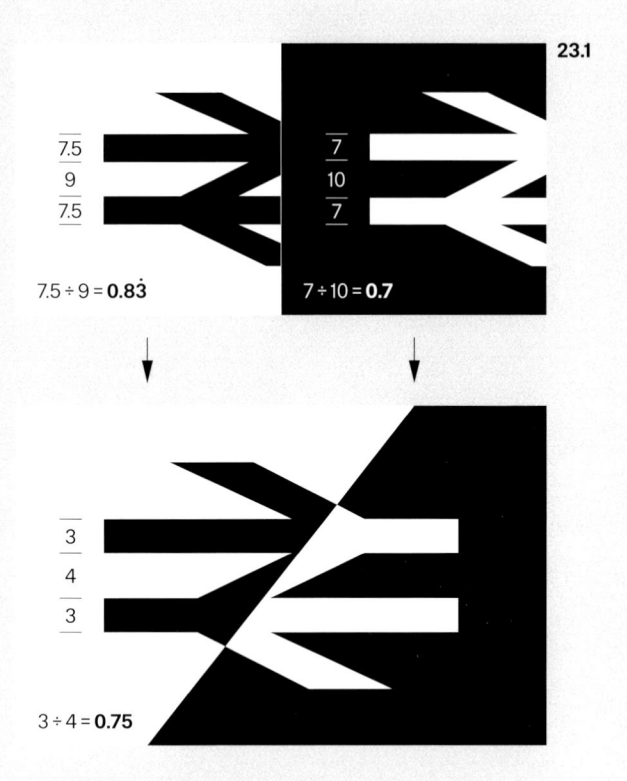

$7.5 \div 9 = 0.8\dot{3}$ $7 \div 10 = 0.7$

$3 \div 4 = 0.75$

An optimum middle ground between the original weights eliminates the vanity of specifying two different versions **23.1**. Whilst this strategy may not necessarily please the purists, this approach would certainly have the desired effect of exerting a greater degree of control upon the application of the symbol across the network, something that is needed now more than ever, when so few appreciate the nuances of optical weights. And if any visual discordance exists between the positive and negative versions, not only is it minor but, since in practice the two manifestations are never seen side-by-side, the point is all but irrelevant.

23.2

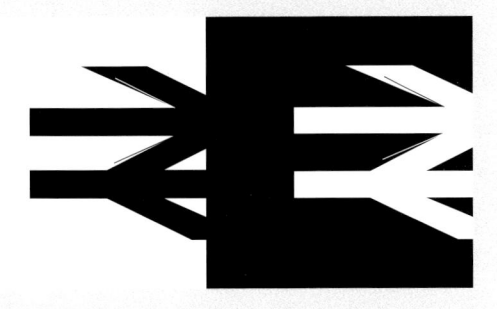

23.3

One of the few occasions for discomfort in the design of original British Rail symbol is the discrepancy between the acute angles of the device **23.2**. Once observed, the issue is hard to put out of mind. Such was the quirky geometry that the disparity is even more pronounced in the negative version, where the inner diagonal is visibly far steeper than the gentle incline of the outer arms. Measurement of the angles in both positive and negative permutations **23.3** confirms that which may easily be perceived by eye. A comprehensive reworking provided the opportunity to correct this imperfection and bring improved symmetry to the diagonal strokes **23.4**. It should be noted that the minor difference between the angles of both arms of the symbol in this diagram may be ascribed to the slight flaring of the arms, a necessary design attribute introduced in chapter 3 and covered in greater detail in chapter 9. This feature was naturally carried forward to the proposed revised symbol.

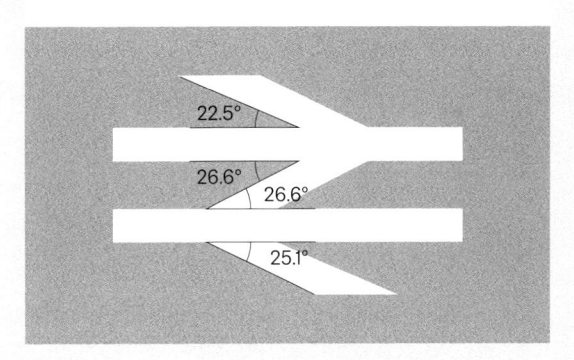

23.4

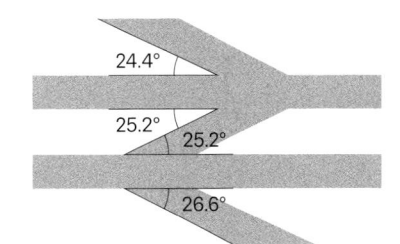

23.5

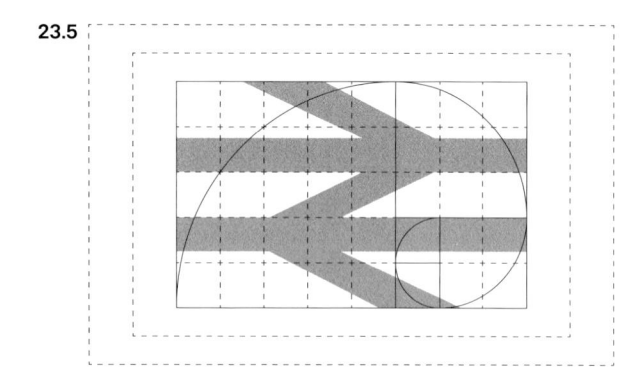

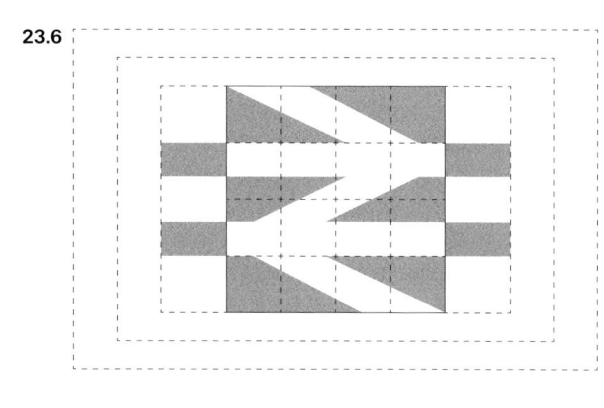

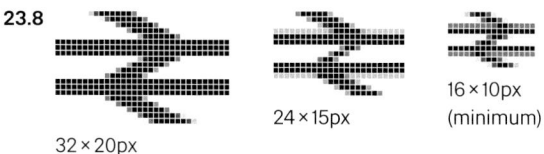

23.6

23.7 4 × 2.5mm   3.2 × 2mm   2.4 × 1.5mm   2 × 1.25mm (minimum)

23.8 32 × 20px   24 × 15px   16 × 10px (minimum)

There also remained the small matter of the unprincipled 38:23 proportions, particularly unhelpful when specifying design sizes. The relationship between width and height would surely benefit from being rationalised, provided the overall ratio could be broadly maintained. Two alternative ratios were explored—5:3 and 8:5—the latter falling fractionally nearer to the golden ratio and proving more beneficial by introducing a more practical and convenient relationship between the two dimensions, all drawn with a respectful nod to the eminent Italian mathematician Fibonacci **23.5**.

Extending the arms of the symbol slightly ensures the point-to-point proportions are perfectly square **23.6**. This imperceptible adjustment makes the revised symbol twice as tall as the horizontal tracks, offering another useful layer of assistance to designers. This modification also enhances performance especially at small print sizes **23.7** and at low resolution in the digital environment **23.8**, scarcely a consideration when the symbol was originally drawn in the mid-sixties.

A series of basic tests on the social media platform Twitter showed a selection of different symbols in both positive and negative formats, including original and proposed symbols. When asked for a preference, the revised symbol returned favourable results, comfortably ahead of both of the original optical variants applied incorrectly, as expected, but markedly also outperforming the correctly applied, original negative version. Respondents thus appeared willing to embrace a heavier negative version; further proof that two versions of the symbol are not all that necessary after all.

Geometry for constructing the revised rail symbol →

| 8 | 8 | 12 | 5 | 10 | 3 | 4 | 3 | 10 | 5 | 12 | 8 | 8 |

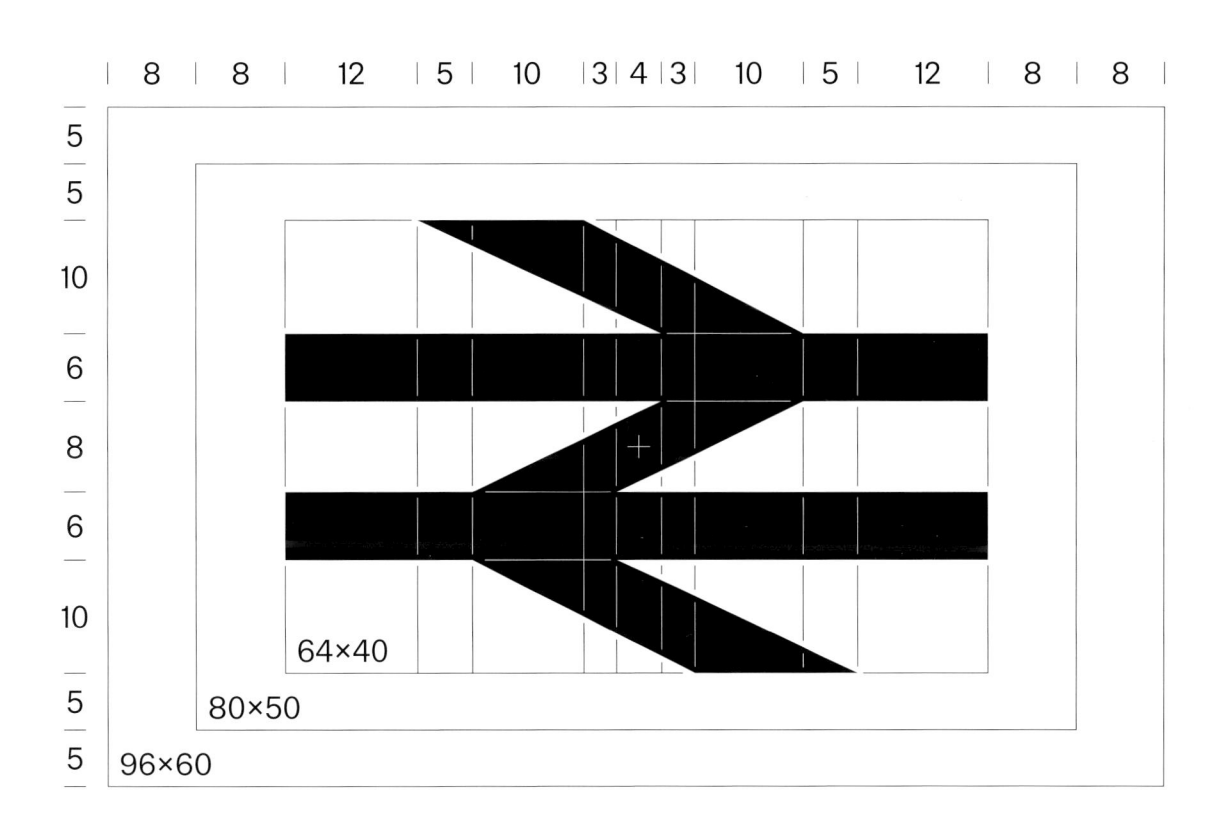

5
5
10
6
8
6
10
5
5

64×40

80×50

96×60

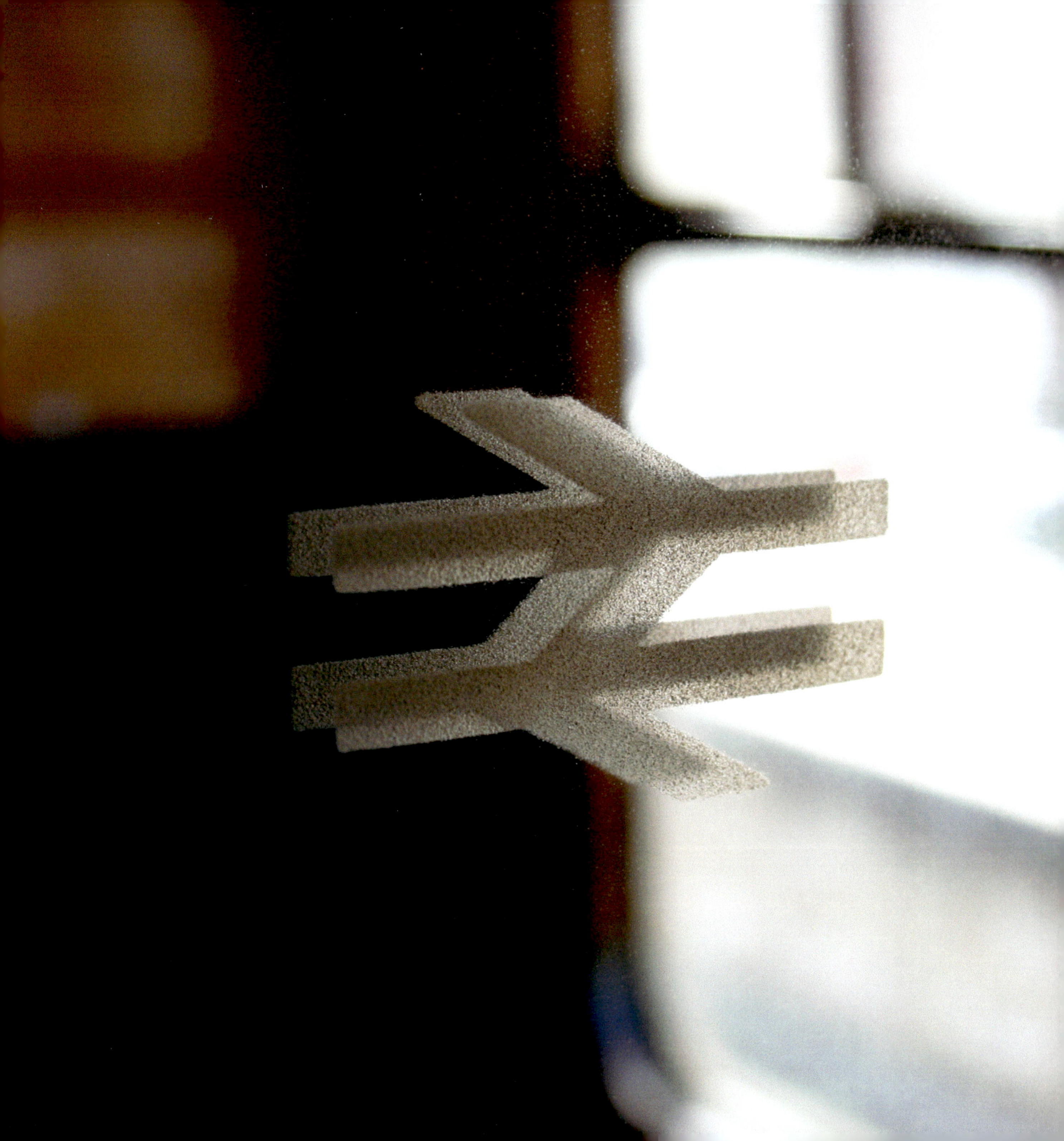

24
Back to the future

Towards the end of the 2010s, some 25 years after the dismantling of British Rail, the visual anarchy across an increasingly disparate and fragmented railway landscape prompted Network Rail to pursue a fresh, joined-up approach to wayfinding.

    More than fifty years after she and Jock Kinneir had fashioned Rail Alphabet, Margaret Calvert was approached by Network Rail to reinterpret the classic for the digital age as part of a bold strategy to overhaul signage across the rail system. Rail Alphabet 2 was designed in collaboration with Henrik Kubel of London design studio A2/SW/HK, with whom Calvert had already worked on a number of typeface projects, including New Transport, which is used for the public sector information website *gov.uk*. The basis of the family was the SIGN Medium weight **24.1** with compact spacing for use on signs, from which a further three TEXT weights in both upright and italic evolved **24.2**, providing a flexible typographic toolkit for Network Rail which has since started to use the typeface in various publications.

24.1

Rail Alphabet 2 SIGN Medium

ABCDEFGHIJKLMN
OPQRSTUVWXYZ
abcdefghijklmn
opqrstuvwxyz
0123456789

24.2

Rail Alphabet 2 TEXT Regular and Italic

ABCDEFGHIJKLMN
OPQRSTUVWXYZ
abcdefghijklmn
opqrstuvwxyz
0123456789

Rail Alphabet 2 TEXT Medium and Medium Italic

ABCDEFGHIJKLMN
OPQRSTUVWXYZ
abcdefghijklmn
opqrstuvwxyz
0123456789

Rail Alphabet 2 TEXT Bold and Bold Italic

ABCDEFGHIJKLMN
OPQRSTUVWXYZ
abcdefghijklmn
opqrstuvwxyz
0123456789

← British Rail Mark 1 carriage mirror with sand-blasted symbol

The government white paper *Great British Railways: The Williams-Shapps Plan for Rail* **24.3** was released in May 2021 and announced the future creation of Great British Railways (GBR), a state-owned, public body to oversee rail transport in Britain, promising, among other things, to 'bring the railways back together'. Absorbing the current infrastructure owner, Network Rail, and various functions from the Rail Delivery Group and Department for Transport, GBR is set to own the infrastructure, receive the fare revenue, run and plan the network and set fares and timetables.

Dismayed by the use of another distorted version of the double arrow throughout the white paper **24.4**, I tentatively reached out to the then chair of Network Rail, Sir Peter Hendy, to share my convictions about the pressing need to re-specify the symbol. I was invited to present my proposal to key stakeholders at Network Rail, who were not only favourably disposed to locking down the symbol but also eager to include the revised design as a core part of a new wayfinding initiative which was in the early stages of development.

And so began the latest chapter in the life of the double arrow—an exciting project to reset the symbol. The design manual for Rail Symbol 2, *NR/GN/CIV/300/05*, was published online by Network Rail in September 2022, produced in close collaboration with Anthony Dewar and Frank Anatole of Network Rail, and Calum Spence of Design Council, The new manual contains extensive guidance covering the design and application of Rail Symbol 2 to ensure a uniform approach across the entire railway network.

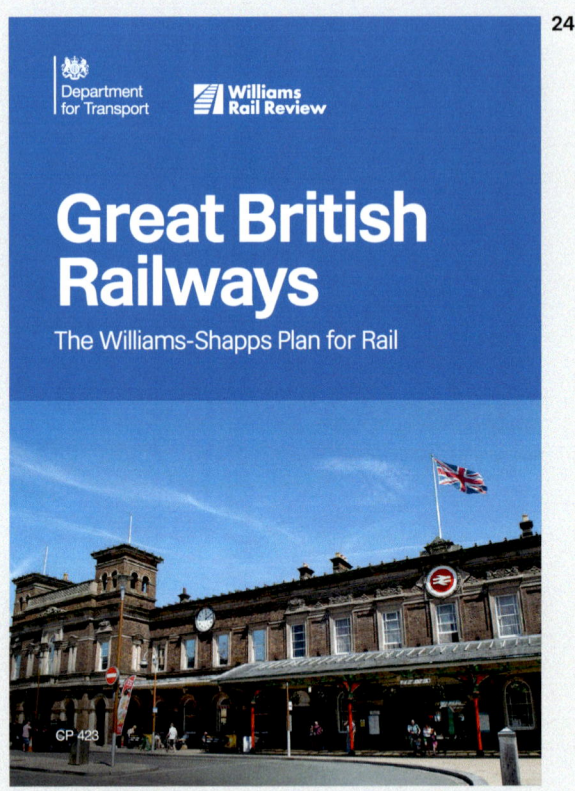

24.3

24.4

Rail Symbol 2 →

Around the time of Brexit (the departure of the United Kingdom from the European Union), Boris Johnson's Conservative government had begun a drive to re-instil a sense of national pride, evidenced by an edict in March 2021 that the national flag be flown from all government buildings. In February 2022, it was pointed out on Twitter by Chris Applegate that Network Rail had registered a suite of three new logos for GBR with the Intellectual Property Office, featuring an insipid adaptation of the symbol used by British Rail International (see page 48), which had previously taken the Union Flag as its inspiration. For those who do not necessarily espouse this particular flag-waving political position, the hope remained that the dark blue constituents of these patriotic but aesthetically unsatisfactory logos could be dispensed with by stealth in the course of time, leaving nothing more than a pure, unadulterated symbol in red. After a somewhat scathing critique on social media, the GBR flag logo was thankfully neither seen nor heard of again and there is little or no appetite from this author to bring it back to remembrance.

Back in October 2021, the then Secretary of State for Transport, Grant Shapps, had launched a national competition to establish the location of the new headquarters for GBR, somewhere far away from London to demonstrate the government's commitment to their 'levelling up' agenda, one of several key selection criteria. Following several months of deafening silence, leading to much speculation in the media that the GBR project had quietly been shelved, it was announced in March 2023 that the new organisation would be based in Derby, one of a shortlist of six locations away from London having a notable railway heritage.

Until July 2024, there was no tangible sign of GBR, nor was there ever likely to be in the closing stages of a Conservative government onto its fifth Prime Minister to have held office since David Cameron was elected in 2010. The last Tory incumbent Rishi Sunak's most recent intervention into the affairs of Britain's railways came in October 2023 with the lacklustre cancellation of the northern sections of HS2 from Birmingham to Manchester and the East Midlands due to spiralling costs, leaving the ambitious high-speed railway endeavour as a shadow of its former self and scant assurance that HS2 would even reach its original intended central London terminus at Euston.

With the Labour Party having secured a convincing majority in the July 2024 general election, the baton has now passed to Sir Keir Starmer. It was announced in the King's Speech on 17 July 2024 that the Labour government would be moving ahead with the formation of Great British Railways and renationalisation. In the run-up to the election, Labour promised change. It remains to be seen if they can deliver the game-changing transformation that Britain's railways so urgently need but initial indications offer new grounds for optimism.

24.5

200
**Years of Train Travel
Since 1825**

What does the future hold? 2025 marks two hundred years since the opening of the Stockton & Darlington Railway. To celebrate this anniversary, the rail industry will be launching *Railway 200*, a year-long nationwide campaign, to inspire a new generation of young people to choose a career in rail. Starting in January 2025, a wide variety of activities and events will showcase rail's remarkable past, its role today, and its importance to a sustainable future.

The Railway 200 identity was designed by global brand consultancy Interbrand and represents the progressive contribution rail has made over the past 200 years to Britain and beyond. The logo **24.5** gives due prominence to Rail Symbol 2 along with a dynamic 'thread' to represent the idea of a continuous, unbroken line that reaches back into the past but is always leading ahead into the future.

With this significant milestone for Britain's railways just around the corner, it seems the dependable double arrow has become impossible to shift. The Railway 200 logo is further proof that, some sixty years after it was dreamt up, the magical symbol has achieved immortality—the mesmerising and elusive substance of which modernist dreams are made. See it at a station near you!

93

Acknowledgments

In addition to Gerry Barney, the designer of the original British Rail symbol, and his associates at Design Research Unit, the author would like to express sincere thanks to the following individuals and organisations, without whom the publication of this book would not have been possible:

Frank Anatole
Mike Ashworth
Luke Davydaitis
Gareth Dennis
Anthony Dewar
Tim Dunn
Jack Hale
Alistair Hall
Ellie Harrison
Peter, Lord Hendy of Richmond Hill
Wallace Henning
Tony Howard
Matthew Murtland
John Oldfield
Mark Ovenden
Gareth Peate
Eddy Rhead
Calum Spence
Peter Thorpe
Chris Timings
Daniel Wright

Bring Back British Rail
British Railways Board
City of Doncaster Council
Department for Transport
East Lancashire Railway
Ecclesbourne Valley Railway
The National Archives
National Railway Museum
Network Rail
Network SouthEast Railway Society
Nottingham Trent University

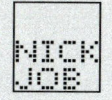

About the author

Nick Job is an independent designer, based in Macclesfield, UK. He has a degree in graphic design from Nottingham Trent University. After a decade as in-house brand designer for a global logistics provider, he launched his own design business, realising a long-held ambition to produce type. He has since released retail typefaces with Monotype, Fontsmith and Rosetta. Nick, a self-confessed anorak, is the author of *doublearrow.co.uk*, the British Rail Corporate Identity website.

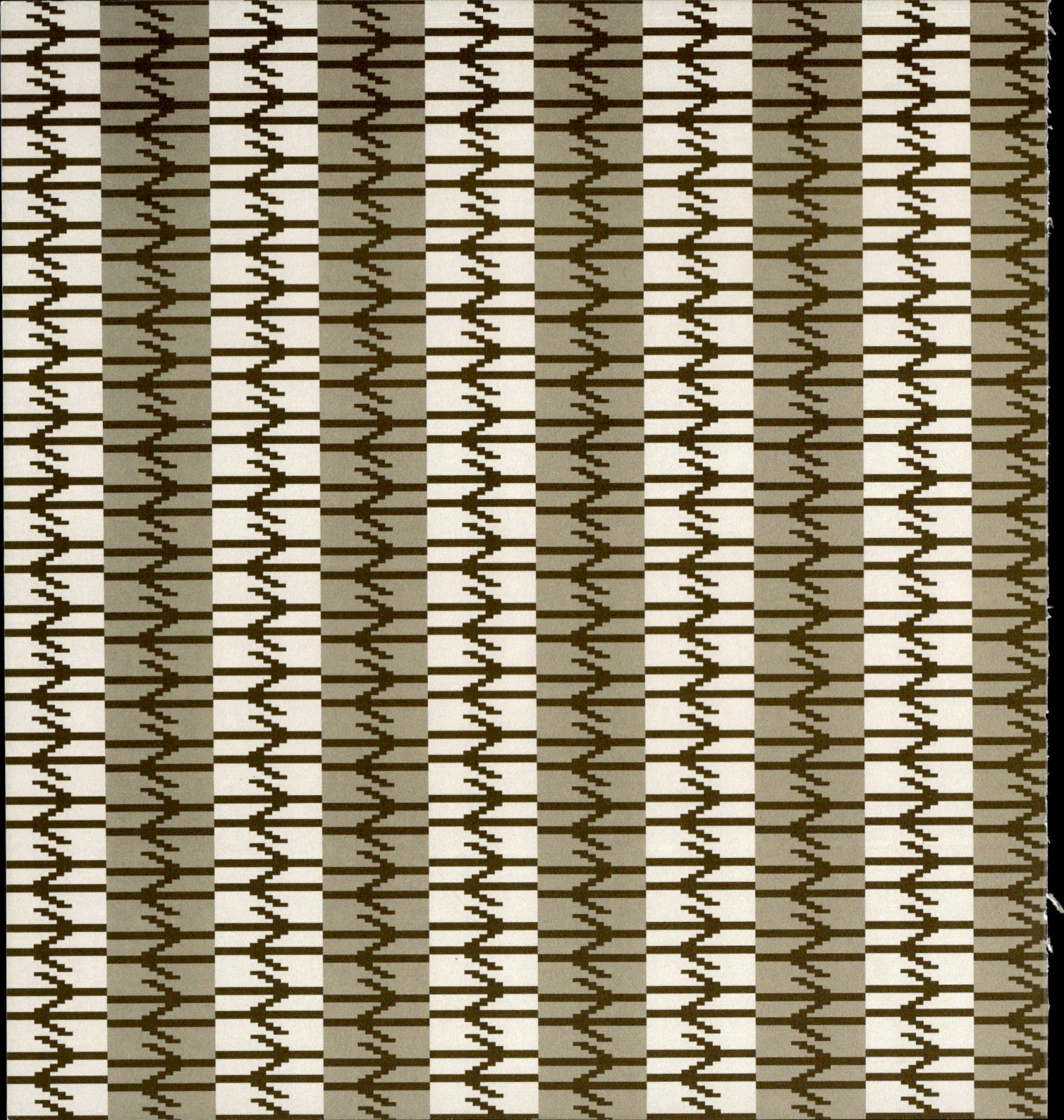